Remarkable Leadership

Easier than you think
Bigger than you can imagine
Straight from the heart

Danielle Macleod

Published by New Generation Publishing in 2022

First Edition

ISBN
    Paperback: 978-1-80369-436-8
    Hardback: 978-1-80369-437-5
    Ebook: 978-1-80369-438-2

www.newgeneration-publishing.com

 New Generation Publishing

Cover Design: Clarissa Design

'If your definition of success has little or no mention of love, get another definition.'

Robert Holden

Dedication

To Chloe, the Warrior Queen choosing continual transformation, even when the sword is demanding you pick it up. I wrote this book for you.

And Ann Hodgson, a Queen of English Language and Literature. You are such a big part of this. Thank you for nurturing my childhood passion. Your legacy shines through those of us lucky enough to have been taught by you.

A note about this book

Remarkable Leadership is written using the feminine noun, 'Queen'. It speaks from the female voice.
Sometimes, it refers to challenges that women face in a different way to men.
Does that make it a book for women?
No.
It is a book about a style of leadership that the world is calling for.
It is about a way of being that is as applicable and exciting for men as it is for women.
You may find it surprising to read a book that is written this way, about this particular topic, in the voice of a woman.
Isn't that worth exploring in itself?

Praise for the Remarkable Leadership Programme
and the methods taught in this book

I cannot endorse the programme enough. Where I stumble is in trying to do it in a succinct way as it has totally transformed every aspect of my life for the better!

Seren Jones, Business Designer, Cloud

No ordinary leadership programme, this year of growth guides us to understand and harness our inner power, love and wisdom; to shift our thinking and aspirations to another level; to come together as a powerful collective and find ourselves capable of changing our worlds. I am forever changed; forever grateful.

Liz Clayton-Jones, Director, Beehive Performance Ltd

The Remarkable Leadership Programme has been truly educational and inspirational. It has opened my eyes, ears, and most importantly my heart. I am retiring my warrior peacefully...I have now found my tribe and am curious about how I can serve my teams.

Cigil Tisdale, Heart Centred Leader, Sales Operations

I have gained so much from the insights and challenges that this programme and community has brought me. It's deep and supportive and I highly recommend it.

Barbara Lawther, Management Consultant and Author, The Watch House

I needed to break out from the repetitive thought patterns that had me swing from childlike victim to against the world warrior. I'm so grateful to have had Remarkable Leadership recommended to me. It has let me unearth the Queen in me whilst giving me peace in all I do. I'm free!

Bayile Adeoti, Founder, Dechomai Ltd

i

Remarkable Leadership has changed the way I lead and the way I live. What is truly remarkable, is how there is something there for everyone. Whether you are a senior leader, new to leadership or don't even consider yourself to be a leader yet, this programme gifts you a new way of looking at yourself and helps you share your talents so you and others can shine. Without question, this programme helps you as an individual but applying its principles and unleashing your remarkable leadership helps everyone around you. THANK YOU!

Lisa Murdoch, Managing Director, Unleash My Future

Remarkable Leadership develops a style of bold, heart-centred, compelling leadership that benefits everyone. It has been absolutely game-changing for me, enabling me to create the kind of impact I want to make in the world. I can't recommend it highly enough!

Helen Arbuthnott, Senior Leader, Financial Services

Joining the Remarkable Women Community and Leadership Course has been one of the best things I have done to invest in myself. It has given me reflection, challenge, space to grow and long-term investment in me and therefore every aspect of my life.

Pam Hunter, CEO, Say Women

The concept of 'Queen Leadership' has encouraged me to subtly change my way of being, aligned to my innate super-powers of compassion and intuition. The impact of showing up in full expression of how I am and having the courage to stand in my truth has been profound. The programme has changed my life – that is all.

Jayne Price, Senior Leader, Innovation

About The Author

In 2016, Danielle Macleod left the corporate world to set up an organisation, then called Somebody Inside, with Nic Devlin. Having started out in life quite clear she would be Prime Minister or Captain of the British It's a Knockout Team, or maybe a doctor, she could never have envisaged becoming a leader of over 10,000 people in one of Britain's biggest corporates. During her time there, she continually explored the idea that there had to be another way to lead. One that achieved results and honoured the whispers of her heart to love more and bring more humanity to a world that seemed to value profit above all else.

She used her later years in corporate life to explore these ideals and to focus on her own inner transformation: to become the leader she wanted to be. The results followed, albeit with the inevitability of her own human transgressions and mistakes. She realised she wanted to teach that work to every woman who wanted to hear it.

In 2018, Nic and Danielle changed the name of Somebody Inside to Remarkable Women, in honour of the many women they had spoken to who were denying their glorious potential. Their decision to surrender corporate life to share the many tools they have learned from a spectacular array of teachers has remained resolute.

Danielle lives in Edinburgh with her husband, John, and a willful yet lovable French bulldog, Jessie. They walk the Portobello beachfront almost every morning to greet the day.

Remarkable Leadership is Danielle's second book. *Remarkably Easy – How to Get out of Your Own Way and Unleash your Brilliance* was released in 2018 by Chaseville Press.

Foreword
Nic Devlin

When I sit to write these words, I've been surprised at the well of emotion that's been stirred. I'm reminded of my own stories, and this book feels like the handbook that I wish someone had put into my hands so many years ago.

Growing up as an only child I often found myself looking at the world, observing, trying to make sense of what I saw. Invariably I looked outside of myself: for validation, guidance, wisdom, and indeed sometimes for love. I didn't know it then, but I was searching for something. I just didn't realise that life was going to bring me full circle, back to *ME*.

When I look back, I can see how in so many ways growing up, we're offered a different handbook. How the people around us shape us and our view of the world. We're all born with infinite potential. Of course we are: our very existence is a miracle. We are all unique beings. Yet the moment we arrive, the programming starts. Like sponges we absorb the rules of the game, cultural norms, a way of being that has us pick up an exquisite code: a bundle of labels and stories that we believe define who we are and, importantly, who we think we're not. Be good, be nice, stay quiet, I'm too much, I'm not enough... the list is endless. We hold on to these ideas and limitations so tightly that we pretend that they're part of our DNA. We put ourselves into personality-shaped boxes and our potential shrinks to fit. We view the world through these lenses and create a reality that matches. Wild, eh?

Then one day, we start to get a sense that the path we've chosen is too hard, that maybe it wasn't a path after all but a cul-de-sac, and we start to feel like we're running out of options. That what used to be fun or effective is just not having the same impact, and our Hearts and our Bodies (remember those) yearn for something different and no longer allow us to distract ourselves with 'all the things'. Put simply, it becomes so tiresome being US that we start the search. This time in earnest. What a wonderful moment… Maybe this is you right now.

My very first memory of a true Queen was my Auntie. Everyone called her that. Though I don't remember the first meeting as a baby, I do recall how when she came into the room, there was that *presence*: calm, capable, strong. She smelled of lavender talc and her piecing blue eyes crinkled with laughter and love. I would sit at her feet, spellbound by her and how life seemed different somehow just because she was there. I didn't know then that as a newlywed bride, her husband had been killed in a mining accident and without his hat, the pit declared no liability, leaving her penniless and childless. You'd never have known. Though she hadn't chosen her circumstances, she most certainly did choose her response. I treasure the times we spent together. Decades later, though the words have faded, I can remember her luminosity, how she made me feel and how the world became more vibrant and alive when she was around. She was a true Queen in every sense. She gave me an incredible gift – it's only now, as I enter my 50s – the 'Second Half', that I can truly breathe that gift in. It's in the gaze of a Queen meeting another Queen. You know.

This is why this handbook is so important. It opens up a whole world of possibilities that up until now you might not have seen. These possibilities will invite you to go inward and find *YOU*. You will be able to nurture your own North Star so that the little whisper that endlessly gets droned out in our younger years, starts to be heard, to *LEAD*. There's a big difference between following and knowing. You will learn to trust your intuition and allow that to be your sat nav and your focus. It's time to honour *YOU* and let that guide your choices. We are all leaders if we choose to be. We all want to see something different in the world.

But how? This book will give you endless tools and techniques, or instead you can make the experience far more profound and explore. Allow the insights in these pages to open you up, to speak to your truth.

Let's imagine a world where every little girl is surrounded by real Queens. Women who can own where they have been and can indeed hold your gaze. Women who are not ashamed to own their own darkness. Women who have wobbled and fallen over; been into the arena and literally crawled their way back out. Women who have learnt that showing up as vulnerable *and* real, with courage *and* mess, with love *and* sometimes a broken heart, is THE way. Women who have dropped being perfect or ready, but instead have chosen to RISE. Women who are not afraid to look to another Queen to help them rise too. Queens don't do it alone – we know that's not the way.

In THAT imaginary world, as each little girl grows up, she learns that her beauty comes from within, whatever her shape or size. That the inner and outer critics may mutter and can never replace her own truth. That her true worth is not up for negotiation or debate. That she was born ready for the path and that at each step she is able to see a zillion other powerful examples of authentic women around her, cheerleading her along the way. Not in their words, for we rarely heed those in our youth, but in who they are BEING. Isn't THAT the world we want to be living in?

Queens know that who they are, their role and that their legacy is important. They show up. They're done with the trivia. They want to LIVE life fully with an open heart. To contribute in a meaningful way. To play their part. To go all in. They don't leave it to others or let fear get in the way.

So, now, YOU. Come and take your seat, knowing a whole new chapter is about to begin. We've been waiting for this moment, for you to arrive. You're right on time. From my heart to yours, thank you for choosing Queen. It matters – more than you can ever imagine. Don't believe me? Look at the world around you.

You, We, are needed more than ever. It's time. Let's do this.

Nic x
Co-Founder, Remarkable Women

'When I stand before God at the end of my life, I would hope that I would not have a single bit of talent left and could say I used everything you gave me.'
Erma Bombeck

Contents

CORE FOUNDATION THREE:
SLOW DOWN TO SPEED UP

THE MOST IMPORTANT COMPONENT

Introduction

Early on in the days of our business, Remarkable Women, Nic and I kicked off a small research project. I wanted to speak to women who looked on paper like they had it all. I wanted to understand whether they were living into their true potential. I wanted to hear their dreams and whether they were realising them. I wanted to know if women really were suffering the 'confidence crisis' that the world kept telling us we were.

I spent hours in deep conversation with brilliant women from all professions. Of those I spoke to, 95% told me that their greatest longing was to 'make a difference'. They weren't all clear on what that looked like or indeed how to do it, but most of them did know that the path they were on was not the one they had in their heads. They had beliefs that were getting in the way.

Interestingly (although not surprisingly to me) those beliefs didn't have much to do with confidence at all. They were more nuanced than that. They centred around the perceived 'cost' of success or making a difference. Statements like, 'I don't want to compromise my health', 'I don't want to modify my values', 'I don't want to mess with my relationships' came to the fore time and time again, along with the simple idea that maybe they would fail. Even the idea of failure didn't seem like a confidence thing, but more that the possibilities and change they could envisage seemed bigger than they could handle on their own.

And so these beautiful, brilliant ideas and desires, that truly had the potential to change the world, were being put on the shelf. To that famous day in 'Julember' when the planets would align, there was enough money in the bank, the risk had been minimised to the point of non-existence and they were finally in control of their lives. *THEN* the change could start. One day. But not today. Not yet.

When we saw such a clear pattern of response, we began to get excited. You see, all of you, whether you consider yourself high potential or not, have insight into the things you'd love to change. In your organisation, community and even the world. Those ideas are too good to be shelved until some imaginary point in the future. That desire is too great to ignore.

We need you in your brilliance. We need you alive to the fact that the greatest thing standing in your way is *YOU*, and that voice in your head that calls you back.

Enter the Queen. A simple, powerful and insightful way of *Being, Doing and Leading* that you can start to use today, to bring those future dreams into the present moment. Bolder than you can even imagine, easier than you think. *I promise.*

It's time to stop convincing and become compelling and inspiring. A truly remarkable Queen Leader.

Let's begin.

SETTING THE SCENE

Chapter 1: Introducing 'The Queen'

The Queen gets a bad rap in mythology. Look around you, you'll see it everywhere. Over the years we have centred many stories on Princesses who need to be rescued and on Wicked Queens who create devastation in their lands. There's always a Prince on his white horse saving the day. It's a clever narrative. And one that needs busting. Fast.

Then there's another problem. The word, 'Queen', as it relates to the modern day. I remember a brilliant woman saying to me, 'I really think you need to change the name, Danielle. I just can't wrap my head around it. There's too much noise in the word for me. I don't believe in the monarchy and I don't want some outdated establishment in my day-to-day vocabulary'.

I smiled. I get it. *Truly.* I also said no.

For me, the Good Queen is a powerful archetype and the one that most easily embodies all that I am about to reveal to you in this book. The Good Queen is a concept that we can harness and use in ourselves to create impact and bold change, every day – professionally and personally. She is the very essence of feminine brilliance: heart-centred, purposeful, vibrant, grounded. She leads with clarity and love. The world is a better place for her contribution.

Over the years we have run Remarkable Women, Nic and I have learned that when we dilute a model so that everyone in the room can 'get along' with it, we dilute the very essence of what makes it so powerful. This means that those who could really benefit from it, miss the depth, vibrancy and clarity that come when something resonates deeply within oneself. The people who it is not for, well, they kind of get it, but it never really gets into their bones anyway. So, now we stay true to the clearest model we know how to create, honing and shaping its edges as we embody it more and more in our lives.

That decision not to dilute our model makes a great first introduction to the inner Queen. You see, she knows that she doesn't need *everyone* to make the impact she longs for in the world. She simply needs those who are ready to hear a clear call to action. Her leadership is not about convincing, it's about standing true for what she believes in.

It's very OK indeed if this model is not for you. And if you're willing, even if there is a little edge in these initial pages, I'd be grateful if you'd stay with me for a little while longer. If you would remain open to the possibility of something exciting and powerful for just a few more pages. If you would adopt the position of *Learner* not *Knower*, just to see if there is anything new for you in the first few chapters.

Why? Because my inbox is full of emails from men and women alike who were skeptical, but who said, 'OK, I'll try', and who later felt inspired to tell me what happened as a consequence. How suddenly conversations became easier, their work became bolder and their lives became more balanced.

I'm asking for a tiny experiment. Nothing more. If at the end, we part ways, then so be it. The world is a better place for leaning into our disagreements and acknowledging them than pretending or wanting to all think the same.

Chapter 2: What About the Kings?

'Yes, but Danielle, we need Good Kings too!' is a conversation I'm invited into repeatedly. YES! We do. This work is as applicable to men as it is to women, so if you're a Good King in the making, then read every page of this book, knowing that there is gold in here for you too, and that we are calling forth Good Kings too in all of our work. I teach 'Queen' on mixed gender stages all over the world, and there are always many men who come to seek me out in the break or who write to me afterwards to share their thoughts and experiences after putting it into practice.

It's worth also noting that the world speaks from the masculine pronoun everywhere (you can tell that simply by noticing what a surprise it can be to find 'she' used in a leadership book – that's because it's not the norm by any stretch). Publishers and algorithms promote books written by men, and the top 20 business books in any regular bookstore will be 80% white middle class male authored. Are they great books? Often, yes. Are there others not getting into that position on the shelves because of years and years of promoting the same thing? *Of course.* I love men dearly – I'm married to the archetypal straight middle class white man and I adore him. He knows as well as I do, that his particular perspective on the world is grossly overrepresented.

More importantly, in all of our research with high potential women we discover a constant theme: that women have more to give; that they truly want to make a difference in their lives; and that the reason they are not *is so much more nuanced than 'lack of confidence'* (in fact, call me cynical, but I happen to believe that tell a woman for long enough she lacks confidence, she might start to believe you). What we see in our research is different. We see women saying they don't want the perceived 'costs' of success: burnout, fractured relationships, risk to security and perhaps most importantly, they don't want to have to become someone they are not to rise through the ranks. They don't want to compromise their integrity or who they are. They don't want to become that aggressive woman who fights to the death to fit in with the 'boys'.

Queen Leadership is all about embracing a different way: about becoming a compelling, rather than convincing leader. Queen Leadership is about recognising that business, fulfilment, leadership are not geared towards 'winning the battle' or 'never giving up'. It's about creating a world where the battles are diffused, before they do damage. It's about creating bold, courageous impact. It's a way that the whole of humanity is calling for.

We start the call with the women. The ones who are already saying: 'This is what we want. Show us how'.

Keep turning the pages. All will become clear.

Chapter 3: Leadership

Let's provide a new definition of the word 'Leadership' in the context of this book too. Because, like Queen, it can get sticky or even exude an air of excluding. Yes, some of you reading this book will be leading huge teams and organisations, some of you will be leading families (even if you don't describe it as that) and ALL of you will be leading your own lives. At least, I hope you are. Because if you're not the leader of your life, who on earth is?

The concept of Queen Leadership is applicable in all of these situations because it's a concept of self-accountability, self-responsibility and self-growth, in service of those who come into relationship with us. Of course, I'm going to share big stories of leadership here. I'm also going to share everyday stories. Because it's how we show up *everywhere* that matters: how we *lead our lives* matters. At the heart of that understanding is bigger transformation than we can imagine.

You can find gold in here if you are willing to apply any of the ideas I'll share with you to circumstances in your own life. Some of you may long for more personal stories. In the end, I simply chose the stories that were familiar to me and spoke best to what I was trying to illustrate. Replace them with yours. Own your leadership role. Who you are matters. What you do matters. YOU matter.

This book is about being the best leader of you that you can possibly be. It's about how everything changes when you are willing to take that mission on. The ripple effect is bigger than you can ever imagine.

Chapter 4: The Three Positions We Can and Do Live From

The basic model I'm about to share will be familiar in some form or other to some of you. Pin back your ears, focus your eyes and open your mind and heart anyway. Sometimes when we spot something familiar, our mind plays a clever trick of making us think we know what's coming. This simple framework is just the beginning. There's so much more to uncover from the three archetypes in this chapter and the way they show up in the world. Let's start at the beginning. As Julie Andrews once sang, in a film that some of us love to sing along very loudly to: '*It's a very good place to start*'.

Position One – The Victim

Victim is a triggering word for many and rightly so. It also offers me the opportunity to get stuck in with a very important disclaimer. *This model is not talking about the extremes in life.* What do I mean by that? I mean that if you are sitting here, reading this and thinking, 'but this absolutely terrible thing happened to me and is she really saying that I created it?' then let's be clear. I am not saying that at all. This model does not apply to encounters with sociopaths, psychopaths, murderers, abusers or any extreme behaviour that you might have experienced in your life. It is not meant for such extremes. There are brilliant people who are trained in the deep work of trauma and that's *not* my field of expertise – it's important that we clarify that straight away.

What the word is designed to do here, is encourage you to take *agency* over the many everyday things in your life that you are contributing to and 'blaming' on others or the world. To show you a way that YOU can empower yourself to create something different, something more aligned with your deepest desires.

That's where we begin.

We can all assume the role of Victim then. Most of us do, more regularly than we like to admit.

The Victim in this model gives away their power and agency, and blames situations in their life on the behaviour of others. Their standard question is usually along the lines of, 'Why does this keep happening to me?'. She often says things like, 'You don't understand, I can't do it because *they* won't let me', or 'If *they* would just stop behaving that way, everything would be fine around here'. Their circumstances revolve around a desire to have others change and do the 'right' thing in order to make their lives easier.

You can see how we get there. It's a place where our mind goes easily. 'If people would just behave the way I want them to, then everything would be great'. It *seems* comfortable to shift the blame for our position on to what others are doing. In reality, that's a deeply uncomfortable position to take, because from a place of Victim, we can only *react* to what is occurring in the world around us. We are literally in a world where we are carrying along, minding our own business and then BOOM, out of nowhere, we get whacked around the head by something out of the blue. We are knocked sideways and immediately struck by the unfairness of it all.

'*Why does this keep happening to me?*' hides a simple truth. If something keeps happening to you (and remember what I said about this absolutely not being applicable in extreme circumstances), the common character in the story that keeps occurring is YOU. It's an uncomfortable place to start. But if suddenly, we change the question to, '*What am*

I doing that creates this?' we find the opportunities to create change, and shift from a position of powerlessness to one of possibility.

The Victim mindset is utterly useless to us. It makes us give away our creativity and inherent ability to create different outcomes from *every single circumstance that is presented to us.* It surrenders our leadership of our own lives, our accountability for what we do and our agency to choose in any given moment. When we find ourselves thinking like a Victim, shifting blame to others and shrugging (or curling up in a ball and weeping) at the hopelessness of it all, the question that leads to the way out is simple: '*Knowing that this is the way things are, what CAN I do?*'

You see, there's no such thing as 'stuck' really. We think there is because our mind loves the simplicity of black and white. The idea that 'it's either this or that, so which one sucks the least?' appears useful and rational, but it isn't true. There are always an infinite number of choices in any given situation. Sure, some of them are ridiculous, but it often helps to remind ourselves in any moment that there must be more options than the ones we are laying out. I'll be coming back to this a lot as we travel together, but for now, let me show you what I mean.

 **Lightbulb Moment: A Familiar Conversation**

You come to me to talk about your options in life. You're tired of your job, but you're scared of moving on, in case what you go to is worse. I smile. I've had this conversation more times than I care to count.

'I just don't know if I can stay,' you sigh, 'I'm getting more and more sick of it by the day.'

I know now to dance with you for a little while, 'So, what happens when you think about going?' I ask (with a fairly strong hunch about where this is headed).

'Oh, I'd love to get a job that I can fly in!' you say passionately. 'But the job market is tough right now, and maybe I won't be able to get that one, or maybe it will look that way but be awful when I get inside, or maybe I won't be able to work in the same pattern I do now or…' You reel out all of the things we all say in this scenario and look at me hopefully as if I have the key.

What you really want me to do is tell you that you should take the leap and that I can 100% cast-iron guarantee that with the right attitude (that we're about to create) and the right actions (that I'm about to share), you can have this *exactly the way you want it.*

I'm not going to do that.

Instead, I look at you and say: 'It's strange to me you believe there are only two options. Stay or go. That your vastly creative mind is literally presenting to you, suck this up, or take the leap, knowing that you could make things a lot worse'. (Sidenote: actually, it's not strange at all. The human mind is pretty much wired this way, but that's a whole new story.)

I pause. Look you in the eye and say, 'What are all the options you have to play with, *right now?*'

You look at me, confused. Your brain does not compute even though you're a smart person. 'What do you mean?' you say. 'I'm here with you, you mean you want me to go and resign right now?'

'You could,' I say. 'You could do a thousand other things too.'

And then we play, with lifting the lid on possibility. In this moment we can easily identify 10 or 20 options that have previously not been on the table. Options like:

- Bringing an end to our session right now and booking a flight to anywhere in the world beginning with the letter 'A' for tomorrow.
- Pulling on your walking shoes and taking a long hike in the country to gain perspective.
- Picking up the phone and calling the first ten people in your phone book that you haven't spoken to in the last month and asking them what they think (even if one of them is your dentist).
- Going out into the streets and running a straw poll from random strangers on what you should do next.
- Deciding that you will simply write your CV to see how it makes you feel.
- Making a single call to a contact you have in recruitment to see what advice they have to offer.
- Emailing five of your most trusted friends to see if they will join you for dinner tonight to bring you their brilliantly funny perspective.
- Going to bed for a long nap.
- Calling your doctor to explain that really, you're more exhausted and anxious than you care to admit and you need to take a rest.

Do I need to keep going?

The Victim lives in black and white. A place where all of the choices suck. Where the best thing to do is stay right here and worry a lot. Probably complain a fair bit too.

There's no wisdom to be found in this mode of being. No freedom. No possibility. It's a trap. When you see it, do whatever it takes to get out.

'They and Them' – the invisible army

When we're in Victim mode, one of our favourite things to do is complain about what everyone else is doing. Or to talk about 'them' and 'they' as if they are real people who are genuinely in our way.

'But you don't understand Danielle, they won't let me,' you say frustratedly. 'I can't do that.'
Honestly, that is so very rarely the absolute truth. Of course, it may *feel* that way, but that isn't the same as it being reality.

The Victim is often trapped in a story of conformity and compliance. This idea that someone else calls the shots. To be clear, most of us aren't *consciously* conforming and complying, but that's what we're doing all the same – following all the rules of how it's supposed to be. What makes matters worse is we are whining about it a lot, whilst arguing strongly for the case that we are indeed trapped and there is no way out.

I can show you a thousand ways this simply isn't true. Let's start with one. As an ex-HR professional, I see it often – it's common for women to come and talk to me when things have got really sticky. When we work on their inner Queen, it's amazing what opens up. We'll get to that bit later, but let's start with the 'wake up' conversation first. Here's how it goes:

'Well, I've reached the end of the line, Danielle. I raised a grievance like They told me and now the case is closed. I can't do anything else. I'm so angry and it's so unfair. How can They do this to me?'

'The case is closed?' I ask.

'Yes. I've been through every element of the process. So that's it.'

I lean forward. 'Honey, nothing is "it" until you decide that it is. Conversations don't end because a flow chart says they do. They end because you have made a decision that this is where it stops. Is this where you want it to stop?'

Let me be clear, am I saying we should fight things to the death? Absolutely not. I am saying that *you get to decide the action you take.* That week off sick that you 'can't take because They will use it against me…', that conversation you can't have because 'They will mark my cards forever', that action you can't take because 'They won't let me' is simply a way of stepping back from your own fear and getting comfortable in blame.

When we step out of the role of Victim, we realise we own the actions we take in our lives and we wake up to the miraculous fact that we get to *choose* the next step in the dance. What others do is up to them. Sitting complaining and longing for others to change gets us exactly nowhere.

If only 'They' would change…

I read this brilliant story once about a minister who had a simple test on whether he would marry couples who came to him to conduct their ceremony. He would spend a little time with them trying to understand whether they were truly in love with the actual person they were in a relationship with, or really operating a covert plan to shape them into the person they wanted them to be and believed they could be. He didn't marry those who made it clear they were hell bent on changing each other, even if they hadn't really acknowledged it to themselves. (As an aside, I wish I'd known about this test when it came to my first marriage. I suspect both of us would have had a dawning recognition that we were better suited to other people in the world.)

Realising that the *only* person we have any power to change is ourselves, is one of the biggest steps we can take to move ourselves out of Victim mode. It's astonishing to me *just how often* almost every one of us believes that if only the other person would change, if only they would be the person we see they could be, if only they would stop doing this or start doing that, then everything would change. Then we *put all of our attention on talking about why they won't change* or trying to coerce them into changing.

It's hard enough changing ourselves when all the agency and choice sits with us. What on earth is it in the human psyche that makes us believe we can change others? You know the quote: 'You are not a tree. If you don't like where you are, move.'

I know for sure that I haven't written enough yet for this concept to land fully with you, even though I suspect and hope, you have heard it many times before. Why do I know that? Because I catch myself in the trap of trying to change others more times than I can tell you, and it's a conversation I have with clients *every single day.* So be warned, I'm going to say it again as we work through this model. And then I'm going to say it a few times more.

Sitting and complaining about others is just shouting from the sidelines of your life and wondering why it's not changing. For some of us it can be so subtle and so ingrained that we don't even notice we're doing it, but we are. The only person whose actions you have control over is you. Everyone else is living their life according to their own motivations and honestly, *they don't care about yours, any more than you really care about theirs.*

If you want to change the way life is flowing, YOU make a change. When you spot yourself in Victim mode, even if you've been there a while, smile, acknowledge that this experience is human and then shift to what you can do to create a change.

Ah, but I don't do 'Victim'...

I really didn't recognise this mode as one I spent much time in when we began to teach this model. In fact, I used to be a little smug about it. I didn't say it out loud, but in my head, I'd be smiling to myself, thinking this was not a place I often found myself. Nodding away, remembering all the people in my life who like to live from the Victim position. Not me though. No, no, no. It's not true of course. If I look back over my life, I can remember many, many times you'd find me in the work canteen with a cup of tea in my hand, earnestly speaking about what a pain in the backside someone else was. If only they would sort themselves out, then my life would be so much easier.

The Victim mindset spends a lot of time in 'if only', because really what's going on is that we are rejecting what's occurring now, surrendering to helplessness and waiting with a sigh for things to change. So, in case you're a little like me and thinking this one isn't you at all, I'd truly invite you to go again and explore. It's helpful for all of us to see there are times we are passively and frustratedly waiting for others to get their act together, or for things to change. The more we are able to see it, the more we are able to do something about it. And by do something about it, I mean make *a choice for ourselves*. In case you were wondering.

Position Two – The Warrior

Position number two is a dear friend of mine. In fact, she worked very well for me for a long time. I might have argued she was the secret to my success. Or so I thought. Meet your Warrior. Her favourite line is: *'I'll beat this if it kills me!'* She's also fond of *'Suck it up!'* and *'I've got to see this through to the end'*. Powerful, assertive and strong.

We'd be forgiven for thinking she's a great one to draw on when we need to make things happen.

Here's the thing though: *the Warrior is trained to die for her cause.* Breathe that in for a minute, because I suspect you may have missed the significance.

Warriors are literally trained to give up their lives for whatever they have decided to fight for. Let me share a secret with you, your Warrior is highly likely to be so overused in your life, that you haven't even noticed that she's willing to 'die' for all kinds of things, almost all of which are not even remotely worth fighting for. Those of you who really won't have noticed are probably thinking you don't 'do Warrior' (just ask Nic, she had this belief for a long time, a bit like I did with Victim), but you do, for sure you do. Any time you take on a cause, or insist on offering the skin off your back to get something done, your Warrior is part of the conversation. If your start to a holiday is pure exhaustion or you often get sick on Christmas Day, there's a Warrior in the mix.

By her very nature, the Warrior is 100% dispensable. That's quite literally the point of her existence. When she dies, she is replaced with another and so the cycle goes on. People energetically giving their 'all', charging through, getting 'what's right', regardless of the impact on others. Creating collateral damage for the sake of 'the right thing'. The formula she uses for success is terrible. Chances are high that you've played the role yourself, countless times.

You'll know you're in a meeting with a Warrior (or two) when the decisions made are essentially about who wields the most power, rather than who has put forward the most sound proposal. Metaphorically speaking, there will be dead bodies and injured people lying around the room. It's more than likely you'll have lost an arm and a leg yourself, whether you win or lose. You see, if she has skills, the

Warrior often wins (that's why we believe she's so useful), *but it doesn't come without a significant cost* – to themselves and to those around them. And wow, has she been trained to think it's her moment to step up WAY more times than she should.

In fact, if you're really leveraging this model, you'll be saving the Warrior for actual life and death moments. Sure, if someone is truly threatening your life (by that I do not mean, about to make you redundant, I mean holding a knife to your throat) or that of your family, by all means fight to the death (although even then, there might be moments for your Queen to offer a different way). But fighting to the death over the Christmas party budget or whether a project goes live on Tuesday or Wednesday? That's a daft use of energy and you can have far bigger impact utilising your Queen.

Often women come to me and say: 'But you don't understand, Danielle, my Warrior gets things done', or my particular favourite, 'I know you say not to use her, but *this time* it was necessary.'

I do understand, I promise.

My aim here is to show you that she doesn't really win at all, and to get you to tune into who you truly want to *be* in the world, as well as what you want to do. The Warrior's energy is all about *convincing* – she's often busy assertively making it clear she knows best and pretty frequently telling people to just get on with it. Controlling and commanding. The shining example of Just F*ing Do It. The consequences of that? People don't want to be led by you really, because they know you'll sacrifice their health and personal relationships in the same way you do your own. They get weary, start gossiping, perhaps even contrive to bring you down a peg or two. The Warrior leaves a trail behind her. It's not usually the one she intended to, even though she might say she doesn't care about what others think. What she doesn't realise is that it's going to be one war after another – until another Warrior defeats her. Which will happen. One day. There's always a stronger Warrior somewhere out there.

Let me be clear too, I'm no angel here. I've been resting my Warrior for many years and it's amazing how many times she pops up her head, alert and ready for war. Do I let her take the show sometimes? Of course I do – I'm human after all. The good news is though, the more you try Queen, the more you realise the way of the Warrior really is the hard way. That knowledge will make you want to practice more and more. Combining Queen life and leadership is compelling. You simply need to try it for yourself.

We'll come back to your Victim and Warrior many times through the course of this book so that you can see these positions in action (and get really clear when they're showing up for you). Firstly, I want to offer you an easier way – the way of the Queen.

Position Three – The Queen

If the energy of the Victim is largely *complaining and blaming*, and the Warrior *convincing and charging through*, the Queen presents in the world as *grounded, compelling and inspiring*. She is so solid in who she is and what she is creating that others are often magnetically drawn to her.

Pause for a minute and play with the question that Nic and I often ask when we teach this work. It's always easier to work with real life examples, and whenever we work with groups, it usually takes just a few seconds for some familiar names to emerge. Think for a minute about the women in the public eye who you know are filled with authenticity and integrity; who are clear about what matters to them and deeply compelling. Those who show up in the world in a way that has you believe they are fair and good – the women you admire deeply and would love to have in your circle, who you know would always act with a clear and considered sense of what's right and who also have clear boundaries. They wouldn't declare war, or be interested in it, and yet, somehow you know you wouldn't mess with them. They would stay strong in who they are.

These women might be corporate leaders, politicians, authors or actors. I'll give you some names here and of course, depending on the country in which you live, you will have your own. Because our work is largely in Europe and in the US, we see similar names each time we speak to this.

Our women almost always offer names like Judi Dench; Jacinda Ardern, the 40th Prime Minister of New Zealand; Michelle Obama and Oprah Winfrey. Brené Brown is another popular choice. Sometimes we get stuck in juicy debates about whether other names that are put to us are really centred as Queens or in fact are more in Warrior mode – it's often a test to see whether some are inclined to lash out or lose their balance on key issues. These don't have to be your names, and you certainly have no requirement to agree with them, I'm simply offering you examples so that you can start to spot the defining characteristics as we outline the Queen archetype more. I'm also aware you will almost certainly want to circle back on Warrior and whether the characteristics are as undesirable as I mentioned. We'll keep covering that as we go through. But for now, let's stay with who the Queen is in her fullest sense of self.

The role of a Queen

Real Queens have nations to rule. Good Queens are focused on the wellbeing of their nation, on prosperity and fairness for all and developing and maintaining a peaceful, evolving state. These are no small things to take on, and the Queen knows the role is complex but clear. Her attention is on her people, her mission, her role. Her actions affect many, her legacy is important and she knows that her levels of energy and vitality are crucial. She knows she cannot create this on her own and that she must draw wise counsel around her, people who will not collude when she finds herself in Victim or Warrior mode. She's clear that she must develop mastery in the things that matter. She cannot 'sweat the small stuff' or allow herself to be swayed by the noise in her head that will misdirect her with its upper limiting beliefs or fear and anxiety about what might go wrong, or what people will think.

It's a huge role. There is no bigger. The Good Queen knows that the best way to fulfil it is to be innately aware of her own sense of self and how she is inclined, (like all of us humans) to self-sabotage. She knows that to really live out this purpose, she needs to create her way of showing up in the world that brings ease, grace, joy. It cannot be a daily struggle where she plans the day of retirement with longing.

The Queen must bring vibrancy and love of life to *today* and *each and every day* in order to fulfil her true potential.

But I'm not a 'Real Queen'

If you're human, like the rest of us, maybe you read that short paragraph and started to wonder if this book or model is relevant for you at all. After all, technically speaking, you don't have a nation to rule, 'subjects' are not dependent on your wise guidance – it all sounds a bit too grandiose when you really just need to pay the mortgage this month, deal with your emails, and make sure the kids have matching socks on.

Stay. I'll join the dots for you. We have more to uncover here.

But for now, tune into that inner longing you have to make a difference. Notice how you hold back because it seems too hard, or not fun, or you don't want to be in toxic environments or you can't trust yourself to spend proper time with your friends and family. Notice how you actually quite like your Warrior and you're building a list of things that say, *'Yes, but these things really are other people's fault'* and stay. If you can (and this takes some awareness) notice how you might even be reading this and thinking, *'I get this, I'm doing it already'* and ask yourself, with loving kindness and an excited sense of possibility, *'Where am I not?'* Imagine for a minute, what it would be like to understand how to live from a sense of fully authentic self, to be tuned in to a mission that fills your soul AND to feel vibrant, energised and joyful. To know that you are more than capable of creating a life for yourself that meets the calling of your soul to create change in your own way and be truly in alignment with how to live your own life.

Imagine that. Quite something, eh?

Wherever you're at in your own Queen journey (even if you've never called it that before), there's more. To get there it might be sticky sometimes, but I can unequivocally promise you that the more attention you give, the more you practice and hone, the more life will reveal itself to you, in glorious unexpected ways. Knowing how to embody your Queen takes practice, self-awareness, curiosity and commitment. The returns, well they're something else indeed and, the good news is, they benefit everyone around you too. Tiny steps, huge momentum.

The statement and the question

The favourite statement of the Queen: *'I create my life.'* Her favourite question: *'How did I create this?'*

The Queen's statement and question form the basis of the three foundations of Queen that we're about to dive deep into. They are deceptively simple, which is why I'll need to repeat them a lot of times for them to truly seep into your mind. If you took nothing else from this but those two simple sentences, you'd have more than enough to work with.

For now, stop and pause. There's a lot to digest here and a quick skim read isn't going to cut it. Grab a pen and start to use this book as a living document if you haven't already. Circle the bits you'd be questioning me on if I was in the room with you. Highlight the things you know you want to sit with for longer. Even you, the one who is hungry to see what comes next and who can't resist turning to the next page.

You see, the Warrior is in a rush, the Victim skims by because she doesn't want to see what's in front of her, and the Queen? She knows there's gold to be mined for. And even though her Warrior is constantly calling her to push through, she is committed to learning how to create space. How to Slow Down to Speed Up. Let this book be messy! Scrawl on it. Highlight it. Use the blank spaces for your own reflection. Let it breathe with you. Make it your interpretation. From here onwards, let's create together.

Go on. Get the pen. (I know you didn't yet). We have time, and this is part of your training.

Chapter 5: The Queen as Creator

Let me confess, one of the traits of my work is that I can sometimes teach too quickly (which is ironic given that one of the core foundational principles of Queen, 'Slow Down to Speed Up', forms a huge chunk of this book). Often, I think I have said something so many times that I must not say it again, in case I bore people. The voice in my head has me imagining that you are sitting in front of me saying, *'Get on with it, we've got this bit already!'* This is exacerbated by the fact that I have taught Queen to literally thousands of women. *'Don't repeat yourself, Danielle'* is a statement that does not serve me well.

For clarity, and to ease my own discomfort, I'm going to make a concerted effort to repeat myself *a lot* in this book. Yes, of course, I'll say things in different ways, and I commit here and now to circling back many times. Why? Because the two statements I have shared with you, 'I create my life' and most importantly, 'How am I creating this?' are truly, all you need to completely shift your experience of almost everything.

What I now know from years of playing with these two statements myself is, simple though they may seem, and even though you may be sitting here right now nodding, thinking, *'This is how I live my life'*, wherever you are with them, there is still *so much more to uncover*. This means we need to sit with them. Unravel them. Poke around in the corners. Ask the questions that need to be asked. Mine them for rich discoveries.

I Create My Life

It's 2022 as I finish writing this book for publication. If there ever was a time in history where many of us might have the right to say, 'But this *did* happen *to* us!' it's now. The whole world is slowly exiting a global pandemic. A new war has begun to add to many other global conflicts. The cost of living is rising dramatically in many countries. At times, the changes felt almost biblical in their proportions. Loss of life appeared random (although in reality is probably much less so when we truly investigate privilege and demographics) and has certainly felt cruel. Business owners saw carefully crafted organisations literally fall apart, while others saw a need for what they offer rocket out of all proportion. As we emerge into the next stage, we are faced with rising food prices, fuel challenges and more. The list seems to go on and on. The extremes are wild and, in many ways, out of our control.

If we look honestly and openly, these disparities have always been so. Extremes have always existed in our world. This pandemic has brought them into new light (as has a new war that is closer to home) because we have not been able to turn away from them in the same way, but they were always there – more predictable, for sure, which in many ways simply meant that some of us did not need to look them in the eye. Now we must.

There has never been a better time in the Western World to see the truth of 'I create my life' – to wrap our heads around the idea that even when life is throwing all kinds of curveballs at us, *we always have a choice in our response.*

The Queen knows that she has more at her disposal than 'suck it up and get to the other side'. *So much more.* She also knows that it would be madness to attach her happiness and her sense of self to things that will pass: the size of her jeans, her job title, the number of rooms in her home or indeed, yes, even this one, the amount of money in her bank account. Why? Because all of these things are fleeting. This time in history has shown us that things can change *in an instant*, despite the most careful planning imaginable. There is no certainty. There is no 'thing' that will keep us safe or steady. The Queen knows beyond all doubt that in any moment, she has many choices. Realising the truth of that holds the keys to her constant freedom.

If the international economic circumstances or a global pandemic feels too big for you to grasp right now, let's move to an everyday concept that absolutely demonstrates that 'things that happen' are, at best, a 50% contributing factor to the way in which we experience life. How each and every one of us *responds* to what happens is the huge variable. And that one is very much in our control. It's the premise at the heart of 'I create my life'. What I'm saying is that we can all experience *exactly the same external incident completely differently.* On one level we all know this. But like the many things that really hold the keys to the way life unfolds for us, we don't often process it in a way that's truly useful. Most of us, rarely own that we are the creators of our experience.

 ## Lightbulb Moment: Same Story, Different Lenses

Imagine you and I are going to see a film at a cinema together. We sit next to each other in the same seats (I'm a fan of the ones that extend out and you can lie down in) and the film comes on. *We are both watching exactly the same thing.* However, even though we rarely give any attention to this, we are interpreting and experiencing the film through our own lens of life.

One example of this difference in lenses is that I decided a long time ago that I would not watch gratuitous violence on TV, curious to see what impact it might have on my mental state. What that means for me is that when something violent appears in a film, it has a visceral effect. It's shocking to me and it can disturb me quite significantly, because I'm not used to seeing it in the same way I used to (my TV used to be stacked with recordings of various murder and crime shows). Previously, I would have processed such scenes as a necessary part of the plot, but now the violence is somehow more real, more brutal. If you are used to watching scenes of this nature, they may have very little effect on you at all. You might even wonder at my strange reaction.

And that's just *one lens*. There could be hundreds of variables in that film. Someone could have an accent that reminds you of someone you fell out with, it could be filmed in a place that reminds you of your childhood, the theme music could evoke memories of a treasured relationship, the list goes on and on. Your mind is processing based on your life experiences; the stories you have built up over time, the things your parents taught you, the range of your education, the subliminal messages of the society you live in.

The Queen is aware of these layers. She's committed to increasing her range of self-awareness so that she can offer herself different perspectives each time something arises in her life that she would not choose. Because it's in understanding the myriad of responses that are available to us in any given moment that we avoid our habitual responses. The ones that if we really thought about them, we would not choose any more.

There is always an opportunity to create something different. Even when we are seemingly presented with exactly the same ingredients as everyone else. Even when we believe we drew the worst lot.

How Am I Creating This?

It can be really hard to create change in ourselves – all of us have a bit of a hit and miss track record. Even those of us who believe we are the most self-aware on the planet, must acknowledge that there are times we simply don't understand why we do the things we do. It's pretty funny really, given that we don't fully understand the single personality that we *are* literally the world's leading expert in (our own), we regularly remain steadfast in the belief that we can change other people, and that we know *exactly* the change *they* should be making.

She may not like it always, but the Queen has reconciled herself to the fact that if she really wants to change the way things are occurring in her life, she needs to turn her attention away from what others are doing 'wrong' and instead explore the eternally challenging question, *'How am I creating this?'*

Let me be honest, if you're anything like me and the many thousands of women we have worked with at Remarkable Women over the years, I'm anticipating it is going to take you a while to get this. You might even be frowning at the page right now thinking, *'No, not me, Danielle, I totally get what you're saying, it's simple enough',* and yet still it's going to take time – because of the love/hate thing most of us have going on with it.

You see, it's powerful to realise that you are creating everything. It's also humbling and annoying sometimes. Most of us have had a lifetime of pointing the finger at others, and sighing and wishing they would get their act together. *Especially those of us who think we don't do it at all.* I see you… At least, that's how I experience it. It's literally my favourite question in the world for creating change, especially when I'm sharing it with clients. When I find myself in a sticky situation and need to turn it on myself, on the other hand, I don't like it very much at all. Even now after all this time.

Yet, I promise, on the other side of that question is pure gold – which is why I offer it as literally the *only* question the Queen needs to ask when she finds life is not coming together the way she wants it to.

 Lightbulb Moment: Creating a Problem

Let me share a moment in my professional career. I had been in my new job for maybe a couple of months when my mentor, the COO approached me at a conference, 'We'd like to get you media trained, Danielle,' he said to me, 'Soon.'

I puffed up my chest with pride. '*Ah yes*,' I said to myself, '*I am glad someone has noticed I am most excellent on camera. I will be good at this. This will be fun.*' I agreed with a smile and patted myself on the back for the great acknowledgement of my inherent talent.

I swear he didn't mention the bit about me actually appearing on a well-known fairly aggressive consumer affairs show two weeks later, defending our organisation against three brutal complaints. (I'm sure he must have done looking back on it, he took such care of my mental state throughout the grueling process, but it was a shock when I received the invitation to be trained *in order* to go on that particular show.)

Anyway, one of the complaints was a royal mess. One of our customer team advisors had agreed compensation with an angry and very difficult customer – compensation that was dramatically in excess of what we would ever offer. That would have been bad enough, except then a well-meaning person in the finance team decided said customer advisor then had to ring up the very angry customer and say they couldn't have the money after all because, well, it was just too much. From that second bad move, we had an imploding PR disaster.

It would have been super easy to divest myself from any responsibility for any of this, given I had only been in the role a matter of months (and frankly, it wasn't even my team who had made the decisions, it was another area of the business), but I was curious about how I was part of the problem, and had perhaps even created it.

I saw it clearly in minutes. The crash was inevitable. You see, we had a motto that we shared across all of our operations that was simple and clear in its brilliance (so we thought). 'Do the Right Thing'. Except, the thing was *both the advisor and the finance person* believed they *were* doing the right thing. It's just on the outside looking in, it was clear both those moves were very misguided indeed.

And if I got really honest with myself, I could remember many conversations in board rooms with my colleagues, debating over similar issues on a bigger level. *And we couldn't agree either.* So actually, there was no wonder that our people at the front line had no idea what *the right thing* was to do, because each area was interpreting the meaning of the phrase from their own particular lens. The advisor wanted to make an aggressive customer go away peacefully. The finance person wanted to protect the finances of the organisation. Both were legitimate stances in their own right. Together, however, the result was disaster.

We had created the problem. *And I was right at the heart of it.* Sitting in many conversations that we simply agreed to stop talking about because it was too tiring to try to find agreement. No surprise then that this rippled throughout the organisation and that I found myself on National TV apologising profusely for our terrible choices.

You might feel I'm being hard on myself there. I want to assure you I'm not. Actually, it was a very liberating moment to discover the opportunity for real change – to realise it was time to stop pointing the finger at the various teams at our front line and to take ownership for my own actions. It gave me the opportunity to model what I was asking for from others and to acknowledge that the practical application of 'Do the Right Thing' was much more complex than we had made it sound.

I was exhausted from the hours of training and filming to go on the show (three days and four and a half hours of filming for a three-and-a-half-minute segment), but I was really quite excited at the opportunity I saw to show up differently. In fact, changing what I did every day was a LOT easier than trying to educate 10,000 people on the things *they* should change…

There are so many places to play with the question: 'How am I creating this?' The more we are willing to bring it out of our toolkit when we are experiencing frustration, fear, anger and resentment, the more we have at our disposal to create immediate change. It's a powerful tool in the middle of an argument when you're defending your position and tensions are escalating. Because what you'll see in an instant is that your mind has resorted to justification, to being right, to inflating the 'goodness' of your position and the 'badness' of the person sitting opposite you. You'll see your deep desire that they change with no desire to change yourself. It may sit uncomfortably with you at first, but once you've seen that what you DO have the keys to – your own actions – have the power to change the situation, there's no going back.

I want to break that down more for you. You see, I've been in hundreds of conversations where people sigh and say, 'But why does it have to be me all the time, Danielle? Why do I have to be the bigger person?'

My answer is simple. 'Because you don't like things the way they are.'

I've quoted this before: 'You are not a tree. If you don't like where you are, move.' It is that simple. The situation is causing you pain. You want to experience something different, so it's time to BE different and to DO different. If you are in a tango with another person and you choose to change your footsteps to a waltz, the dance has to change, because you have changed it. If you spend your time continuing to tango whilst pointing out to the other person that it's time to waltz, well, there you are, still tangoing.

Choose *something* different. *Choose* to see your part in the situation and change that.

By the way, *that's not the same as submission, or surrender.* Nor is it abdicating the role of others in any situation. I'm not asking you to roll over here and pretend things don't matter. I'm asking you to see that you have a part to play in creating something new. And to acknowledge that it's the *only* part you have any control over. You can change the situation immediately. It simply takes a willingness to ask the Queen's Question and to sit with it. Even when you don't want to.

The Way to Ask the Queen's Question

Nic and I have been teaching this work long enough now to know that there are some of you who will fall into a trap of the Victim when asking the Queen's Question, so let's nip that fun little habit in the bud right now.

You see, you have to *ask the question like a Queen*. What do I mean by that? I mean that some of us who particularly love to self-attack can use this question as another weapon with which to beat ourselves up. The Victim in us is not really interested in how we're creating anything at all. Which means if we ask the question from her attributes, we ask the question with a long weary sigh, and a sense of, '*I know, it's all my fault again. I really am useless, aren't I?*'

The Queen's Question is an opportunity to create something different and find new perspectives, approaches, experiments and solutions. It's not another stick to attack yourself with. The Queen is never looking to apportion blame – she knows it's a waste of time and energy. She's looking for new ways to view the problem, new modes of action that are literally right in front of her waiting to be taken. She knows the question is often edgy, because it makes her turn the mirror on herself, but she also grows to love it, wise to the knowledge that it presents an incredible opportunity to access new paths.

So, no beating yourself up. If you find that you're about put a heavy load of blame and judgement on your own shoulders that will inevitably lead to feeling stuck, congratulate yourself for spotting it, and go again, *seeking the opportunity to create.*

The Powerful Follow-up Question

Sometimes 'How am I creating this?' has too much emotion in it. There's already fear or anger raging through us, we're finding it hard to lose our desire to blame others and we need another question to help us move into a new space.

Sometimes then, we need a second question. This one couldn't be simpler: *'What would my Queen do?'*

If you can't own Queen for yourself just yet, 'What would a Queen do?' may be even more helpful. This question allows us to step out of the problem ourselves and draw on our powerful imagination for a moment. From here, we get to see what a woman entirely grounded in her own wisdom would create, one who had work to do that was truly important and one who cared deeply about her impact on others.

You have the answers inside you. Sometimes it just takes a simple shift in perspective to reveal them.

The Queen's Symbol

In just a few pages, you have the essence of the entire model. We're about to break it down into three Core Foundations that give you more and more access to the strategies and ways of being that support the Queen in creating the life she longs for. Even so, you have enough right now, to get started.

It's my experience that once women hear this model, something shifts almost immediately. Will it be everything you need? No. I've been evolving and working with my inner Queen for many years now and I'm continually surprised at how many new dimensions she brings. However, I do know for sure, that there are hundreds of women in our world who have created shifts knowing no more than you do right now. It's simply a case of applying it. Of course, for some of us, remembering to apply it is where it all starts.

Here's an invitation. At some point in the next seven days, create visual stimuli around you that reminds you to step into your Queen. Change your screensavers, your passwords, write out some quotes that speak to you. Better yet, *wear something that reminds you that you are a Queen in Training.*

I have two rings that represent Queen for me. They are both inexpensive costume jewellery (before you think I'm sending you off to purchase the crown jewels, I bought them both at Camden Market in London – one of those places where you can get lost in shiny trinkets for hours). One is my 'daytime' Queen ring and the other is a very sparkly flamboyant affair that I wear for evening events and special occasions. Neither are anything like any other piece of jewellery I wear. That's deliberate. I want them to catch my eye when I wear them, even surprise me. Some of our clients choose bracelets, necklaces and even bright scarves. I particularly like to wear a ring because I spend a lot of time looking at my hands – typing at a laptop or (slightly shamefully, I'm as human as the rest of us) using my phone. If I put something noticeable on my hand, I can't miss it. It acts as a constant reminder. I don't wear one all the time (that way I find they do disappear from my consciousness as they are so familiar), but they are favourite friends on days I know I need to access more strength.

Find something that will do that for you. Your Queen's Symbol. Wear it for the next week or so to serve as a gentle reminder that you have more wisdom in you than you might remember.

CORE FOUNDATION ONE: PROFOUND SERVICE

Chapter 6: Choices

Now you have the model, we get into the really juicy stuff: the three Core Foundations of Queen Leadership. Before we start, let's go back to that thing so many told us at Remarkable Women when we were researching what would truly fulfil you and have you live up to your full potential. It's about the power of *your choice*.

Our clients told us that they wanted to make a difference. I barely met a woman who didn't throughout the course of that six months of interviewing and frankly, if you've got this far in the book, then I know there's something beating inside you whispering the very same message. Even if you're not clear what it is.

Those conversations told us that many of us are holding back in one form or other – that we have split desires or conflicting messages going on in our heads. Some of us don't believe it's possible to make a real difference without sacrificing things we don't want to let go of, like financial security. Some believe that moving 'up the ranks' means you have to become someone different, lose your sense of self, perhaps even become 'harder' to fit in. Many are worried about the cost to health or even our most precious relationships. We already work really hard and many hours, and that will get worse as we take on more, won't it? Or perhaps you've found a perfect balance of home and work doing something mediocre and a little dull. One way or another, most of us are doing some degree of 'sucking up'. Some are doing a very large amount of it indeed.

The trade-offs may seem too risky, and the cost of making the courageous attempt to dial up your impact may not quite be something you're ready to do yet. You don't trust the system. *Really, you don't trust yourself.*

I get it by the way. These concerns are legitimate. Daniel Kahneman's brilliant book, 'Thinking Fast and Slow' demonstrates that humans are very likely psychologically wired to take action to avoid loss, long before they are excited about the opportunity of gain. We are so afraid of losing, we stay stuck where we are, often having a little moan about it, perhaps feeling guilty that we're not making the difference we know we could, or even daydreaming about that other life.

I'm not a gung-ho risk taker (and nor is the Queen by the way – she has way too much on the line for her 'nation' to lead like a reckless gambler). I don't coach my clients to leap off a cliff and 'hope for the best' without laying the groundwork to understand who they are, the ways in which they will self-sabotage, and how they could leverage their strengths to improve the odds of success. In my experience, there are usually steps along the cliff side, and although tiny steps forward every day might feel like the slowest way to go when we're standing at the top, it's actually a simple case of the old tortoise and hare cliché. Because we could stand at the top of this cliff for hours, weeks, even years trying to pluck up the courage to take the jump, or we could simply get walking, step by step and see what information unfolds as we do.

The Queen is wise. She understands her decisions carry responsibility. She knows, with absolute 100% confidence, that she cannot engineer out risk from her life and she cannot guarantee certainty of outcome. She can be smart *and* good at calculating risks *and* making judgements based on her ever-increasing self-awareness.

BUT.

She cannot choose *how* the game will unfold. *You* cannot choose or control how the game will unfold. You *can* choose who you want to be. You *can* take steps every single day to be more and more of that. You cannot choose what happens and, at some point, things you would never have chosen are going to pop up and show their unappealing faces. That's how life works. We don't get to create a life where we float on a cloud. We learn to accept and ride the waves.

Profound Service starts with a series of choices:
- The choice to take up your Crown and lead your 'nation' by living out your Mission: your way of making a difference.
- The choice to continually invest in your own growth and self-understanding *so that you can be you in your fullest potential.*
- The choice to show up every single day, reaffirming your commitment to live your life in alignment with your true sense of self and your inner wisdom.

The Queen knows that this life is going to take her down all kinds of paths that she might never have chosen. She knows that that is simply the mystery and miracle of life. And since life is going to present her with all kinds of challenges and moments to learn and grow *anyway*, she makes the choice to be all in: to live her life to the full, to give her complete attention to a life truly well lived, to answer the calls of her heart and her soul as well as her head. She makes the choice to discover who she was designed to be in her complete, imperfectly perfect regal glory.

And that starts with Profound Service.

1 + 1 = So Much More than 2

It's a well-known thing at Remarkable Women HQ that Nic and I are not big fans of numbers. We've probably misled everyone a little in that disclosure over the years, so let me make it clearer: we get very little pleasure from looking at balance sheets, profit and loss statements and management accounts. To clarify, that's not because there's no money coming in, or that we don't care, more that we just don't seem to have the kind of brains that understand or pay much attention to squiggles on a piece of paper.

The irony of it is that Nic actually used to work for Inland Revenue back in the day (don't judge her, it's all good) and I have plenty of professional qualifications, including an MBA, that required me to understand enough about business accounting to make sure I got my final certifications. We can do it when we have to, but it's not a place that's fun for us. And it's definitely not an area where we unlock natural flow.

The other thing is, we like to mess with numbers a lot too. We tend to question the rules.
That's why we're huge fans of a formula that mathematically makes no sense at all. 1 + 1 can totally equal 2 if you want it to. I mean, for most of us, that's all it can ever equal, right? But the Queen knows it has a LOT more potential than that.

What do I mean by that? Simply put, there are so many occurrences in the world where the combination of two individual elements creates something significantly more than a 'doubling' of the effect of one.

Let's go to the concept of Yin and Yang for a minute. You know the symbol, it's everywhere, a circle with interlocking black and white tear drops. We take some liberties with our use of it in Remarkable Women to convey a very important message. At its essence, the concept of Yin and Yang is about dualism – describing how seemingly opposite forces may actually be complementary, interconnected and interdependent in the world, while acknowledging that the two aspects coming *together* creates the ultimate balance. In our concept of Queen, we teach it as the ultimate balance of 'Being' and 'Doing'. When these two opposites come together in true balance in our lives, we reach the point at which both are powerful and able to hold each other in their truest impact.

The Queen knows that she must master Being, the inward sense of self, the ability to slow down and be present to what is and the realisation that all is well. The world will turn with or without her. She must bring that knowledge to her Doing, remembering that powerful, focused, clear and energised action can create bold impact. When one of these elements is mastered without the other, we find polar opposites: powerful in their own right and yet, still, leaving questions. Most of us lean one way or the other to some degree. When the two come together we find ourselves in a place of infinite possibilities – able to create bold, graceful impact from a grounded, relaxed, sure sense of self that is at harmony with the world.

In this scenario 1 + 1 creates infinite potential, infinite impact, infinite capability. Yin and Yang is the most powerful example of the formula that the Queen applies. However, she sees that the linear nature of mathematics in terms of releasing potential is limiting. She knows that two people coming together can do infinitely more than two separate beings. The Queen even sees that when she pairs two words together – profound service, ruthless compassion (we're coming to that one) – she can convey enormous meaning and context with very little effort.

The '1 + 1 = so much more' formula is everywhere around you, once you become aware of it. Once you become aware of it you get to start playing with it. Believe me, you're going to get pretty excited at what it creates. In the very best, most creative scenarios, 1 + 1 has the power to equal infinity, which really is something.

Queens in Training

The thing about growing our self-awareness is that it's a never-ending expansion. There's always more. We can allow that to be a disappointing thing: 'I'm never going to get there!' (Victim); a thing we resist: 'This is the LAST time I put my attention on this!' (Warrior). Or we can allow it to be an exciting piece of news that means we never stop growing into our full potential in the very best sense of the idea. Resting in the notion that we are growing (and that we are *always* enough), excited about what we can reveal next. (Queen).

At Remarkable Women, it's pretty easy to see which side of the Yin Yang dimension Nic and I lean into. It's another brilliant example of 1 + 1 unlocking infinite possibilities.

You can probably guess, because I'm the one writing the book, I represent 'Inspired Action' in our world. Nic, on the other, quite brilliant hand, represents, 'Inspired Being'. She's an award-winning executive coach and talent developer who just happens to be a modern-day monk. Yep, for real. The combination we are able to create as a consequence is exciting and continually astonishing to both of us.

You see, if it wasn't for Nic, there's no doubt in my mind I'd be one of those Warrior women burning myself into an early grave (I already have a broken spine and two eating disorders to show for this one), and she'd be still completing that first page of her website that she started 6 years ago... Together, we are committed to finding our balance as individual Queens. Because what happens is, every time I put my attention on mastering Being, my Doing becomes exponentially more focused, clear and impactful (even though every bone in my body wants to ditch the Being and get on with the Doing, because, hey, *we're all human around here*); and every time she puts her attention on Doing, her ability to discern, step into a powerful space and make things happen whilst retaining her sense of Being dials up like a wondrous super power.

We are all Queens in Training.

This means I need you to stop right here and now and truly consider where you fit in all of this.

Either embrace the idea that you are hooked on Doing and kind of know you ought to give *some* attention to Being, but hopefully not too much, because my word does it *slow you down and there are things that need to be done around here, people!* Or embrace the idea that you are paralysed into inaction because of your deep love of Being. Realise that you rarely create the things that seem possible in your mind even though you have a strong inner knowing that you have something special to give.

Whichever half of the circle you live in naturally, the opposite is likely to both appeal and give discomfort to you. Today I'd love you to embrace the idea that on the other side of stickiness and frustration is the sense of wholeness that you are longing for. Understand that the Supreme Doer cannot get to that place by *Doing* more and putting off *Being* until she retires. And that the Supreme 'Be-er' cannot get there either by ignoring her innate capability as a creator in favour of avoiding the hassle.

In that place, that field, where we meet together, we become infinitely powerful. We become the expression of our potential.

The Queen is committed to walking that path.

Chapter 7: Profound Service – a Powerful Combination of Two Words

There comes a point in life where many of us start to question the way our lives have panned out so far. It can come for each of us at different ages, and I guess it's best known as a 'mid-life' point, the moment when we say, '*Is this it? Is this what it was all about? Now what?*' It has been described in thousands of different books and films. At Remarkable Women we choose to think of it as the moment where the ego has fulfilled its needs for security, safety and achievement. We have got all of the 'things' that we imagined were important. We know how to put food on the table and clothes on our back. We've done 'pretty well' in our chosen field or profession, and we've had a few nice holidays too.

Somehow, there's this nagging feeling that keeps repeating itself. A sense of incompleteness, dissatisfaction with the status quo. It's a fork in the road – a point at which we can choose to shoot for even more 'things', thinking that the next promotion, the even bigger car or the even more impressive dream holiday will fill the need.

But, as Dr Tererai Trent says, in her brilliant book, *The Awakened Woman*, it's like we're putting food in the wrong stomach. We're feeding the 'little hunger' and not the 'big hunger'. It's as though our soul is asking for something very different from what our ego wants. Our soul wants to fulfil its potential and purpose. It wants to make a difference in a more profound way. It keeps calling to us, even though we regularly turn away from the gentle prod, feeling it's a big old question that is often just too intimidating to look at.

In our many years of teaching Remarkable Women how to embrace their inner Queen, our clients tell us the same thing. Sure, they flavour it with, 'But I don't believe I can', or 'It's too risky', or 'How on earth would I even start?', but they all come back to a deep longing to make the impact that only they were designed to.

The Queen knows that feeling as the calling to Profound Service – to a life of deep self- understanding – so that she can make a powerful difference in the world, *in her own unique way, against her own wise and instinctual definition of what that means.*

You see, I'm not suggesting for one minute that your Queen has a calling to solve world hunger, or to address global education disparities or to fix the climate crisis. I am saying that inside a Queen is a recognition that she has a role to play, that her life is significant and meaningful, and that the moment she embraces her unique value and talent in the world and turns it to those things she believes are important *and to contributing to them in a way that aligns with who she is at her most joyful, most generous and most complete,* that she steps into a life of Profound Service that she lives easily and happily, because it is at the heart of who she is. A Queen is a human being with a difference to make.

That difference could be as a leader, a mother, an artist, an educator, a conservator, an astronaut, a carer, a gardener … the possibilities are endless and the 'what' is not important. What's important is that the Queen aligns her unique capabilities and talents with the longing in her soul to step up and go 'all in' with the things that matter most to her, without letting all the ways in which she self-sabotages hold her back.

Because here's the thing, going 'all in' is infinitely easier than you think, once you commit. Showing up as your full self is the easiest thing in the world once you try it on and realise it's the suit you were always born to wear. And of course, you're going to fail sometimes. That's 100% guaranteed. But good news, bad news: you're going to fail at some of the things you're only half-assed doing right now too. Wouldn't it make more sense to at least be wholly in the game that matters to you?

It's a path of alignment. When we allow ourselves to be our truest self and honour our deepest knowing, our wise soft voice inside that gently presses us to do and be different, everything changes. The Queen's eye is fixed on uncovering more. A life of Profound Service, joyfully and impactfully lived.

What's the Difference I Want to Make?

It's the million-dollar question, right? At least it is for some of us. For others, it seems a ridiculously easy discovery. I mean, Mozart got going when he was five. That's not typically how it works out for the general population though.

Let's go back to the metaphor of the Queen for a minute. It's important for this whole idea of Profound Service. *The Queen is born into her role. It's a huge role indeed. One day, she will have a nation to rule.* (If I were you, I'd be thinking this book is starting to take a turn of complete madness right now, so stay with me, it's a metaphor remember.)

Whether you believe in a divine creator or not, or anything in between, it's a fact of life that we are all unique individuals in the world. There will never be another me and there will never be another you. We have all been gifted our own unique circumstances and a body, mind and soul that allow us to navigate those circumstances. The gift of free-will says that we can make choices each and every step of the way, so how those unique combinations work together to then create a unique life are, to some degree, situationally and biologically determined. After that, we have a LOT of options in our hands. We get to craft the creation of our life.

Here's another thing that I find pretty interesting. I've yet to meet a person who believes they are living at the upper end of their potential (and I ask people this question *a lot*, it fascinates me). Most people tell me they are living in a range of somewhere between 20–60% of what they believe is their absolute potential. Occasionally I meet a few 80 percenters.

 ## Lightbulb Moment: The True Size of Your Potential

I used to think I was an 80 percenter too. I consider myself to be pretty self-aware and fairly bold in the action I take in this world. *Sure,* I used to think, *of course there's room for more, and I hit the top end of my industry in my career (and I was pretty young when I did it), I've made a difference through lots of fundraising, I've done stuff to be proud of. I'm a good solid 8.*

Oh, how I laugh at that now. In the very best possible way. You see, since I started this dedicated journey of self-awareness, what I've discovered is, *there is so much more to uncover.* If I have the energy and courage for it, I can wake up and view *every single day* to be like Christmas morning. Packed with gifts and opportunities to go bolder, be more courageous, create bigger, love more and be present more to the awe and wonder of what's around me.

Throughout history, humans have done *amazing things.* We have cured diseases that were considered incurable, we have launched rockets to the moon, we have invented television, the internet, penicillin. We have learned to fly. *The only thing that limits us is our insistence that we can't.*

I know that truly understanding what humans are capable of is well beyond my limited imagination. That excites the heck out of me. *Because, what are we capable of, if as an entire human race, we stepped into infinite possibility? What would happen if we all decided to own and maximise our gifts instead of playing them down, pretending we don't have them, refusing to take our tiny but perfectly unique combination and offer it with sincere and excited contribution?*

I know you can see the possibility here. Imagine a world where *every single human being* said, 'I'm here, I love who I am and what I've been given, and I'm going to play all out with joy and excitement every day until I die.'

I promise you, you're not even close to understanding what you're capable of (I don't believe any of us are). It's time to get into your bones that the keys to that creation lie in Commitment, Excitement, Courage, Faith, Curiosity, Ease, Grace, Joy. Especially the ease, grace and joy. They do not lie in Hustling, Striving, Pushing, Obligation, Exhaustion, Sucking Up. Nor do they lie in getting a bigger job title, more money, better handbags and five-star holidays. Those things are just the free toy in the box of cereal. A distracting piece of plastic that you get bored of in no time.

There is so much more.

The Queen makes a commitment to her 'nation' – that she will go 'all in', that she will own her unique brilliance and that she will dedicate her life to serving profoundly AND to creating a life of ease, grace and joy. Because one without the other is yin without yang.

Your path to a life well lived cannot be reached by working harder, pushing more, compromising your health, abandoning your values, or *denying who you are.* To reach that goal, you need to embrace Profound Service *and* ease, grace and joy.

So, without understanding your unique combination, I can't say what it is that you have been designed to do, but I do know for sure that if you commit to getting more and more present in your life, so that you can see the right thing to do in any given moment and do it without hesitation, you will unlock a life that is beyond your human imagination.

3 out of 10 is an amazing place to start. Make the commitment to bring the balance, to reach the heights of profound service and ease, grace and joy. Make the commitment to once and for all getting out of your own way. You have all the keys. The Queen simply honours that when the opportunity arises, she will respond to her bigger calling and ignore her desire to keep herself small.

Chapter 8: Mission – Our Calling

I know that when we teach 'Mission' in our Leadership programmes, there is always a bunch of women who shrink back a little. It's up there with owning our skills as a topic that some of us would rather turn away from.

In my experience, it's the ego kicking in. The voice in our head kicks off with an ongoing mantra, 'Who am I to try and create change?' or, 'I'm too tired for all of that, it all sounds a bit hard', 'This bit's not for me, I'm nothing special' and sometimes even, 'My life's challenging enough already, thank you very much'.

Let's be clear, this is not a book about Purpose, Mission or Calling. That's a whole book in its own right, and to be honest, others have done it much better than I ever would.

But this matters.

It is my experience in my working life that there comes a point for many of us where our soul begins to tap lightly on our heart and head and whisper, 'Hey, do you think it's time to discover what we're actually here for?' Most of us ignore that voice for a while. Head responds, 'Not today, thanks, let's just get the bills paid' and we keep on keeping on, shooting for strange little goals like bigger holidays, a different car or a bigger house. So the tapping becomes knocking. 'I don't think this is the way,' Soul whispers. 'Shall we pause for a minute and check the map?'

One day, having heard the sound for a while, Heart turns to Head, 'I think there's something in this, you know. Why don't we just sit down and hear what Soul has to say?'

Head, still not ready, snaps a little. 'Listen, you dreamers, there's no time for this. I'm working really hard already, there's a deadline to hit on Thursday and I'm giving it everything I've got for us all to get that big promotion. You're worrying about the wrong things. Let me get on with it and stop interrupting. Once we get that promotion, you'll see.'

Recognise the conversation?

Some of you will be experiencing the tapping or the knocking right now. Some of you will be at the loud banging stage. Some of you may have a body or mind that is literally heading towards shut down in order to get you to listen. Some of you know it's time and that's why you're here: reading this, looking for answers.

The Queen doesn't care how big her castle is, because she knows that's not at the root of the life she is longing for. She cares about living a life that she can be proud of and be in love with. She recognises that more things, more holidays, more money in the bank, more job titles or more followers simply create the same results over and over again. More stuff. The knocking doesn't go away. Her eye is on a life WELL-LIVED. She knows that when her heart, head and soul are in harmony, her life can be bigger than she ever imagined. She is deeply curious about how she can make her own unique difference in the world in the most impactful way possible. She is willing to explore her own purpose, create her own mission, respond to the deeper calling.

I know all the objections here by the way, I've been doing this work for a long time. I've worked through most of them myself and our Remarkable Women clients show up with the ones that have never been present for me.

In our society, it seems impossible to believe that we can respond to our soul and keep ourselves secure. There's a 'way' of living that is all planned out neatly. It looks a bit like this:

- Get a job
- Pay bills
- Get a bigger job
- Pay bigger bills
- Plan carefully for retirement
- Retire and realise you don't have the energy to do half the things you thought you would (and wish you had worked out all the other stuff earlier)
- Do some of the things but generally feel a bit confused about it all (and a little bored to be honest)
- Die.

I'm exaggerating to prove a point, but I'm sure you can see what I mean. I remember an old boss of mine with a lavish lifestyle, saying to me once, 'You know I've finally worked out why I have to have all these luxurious holidays and things. It's to make up for all the hours I'm slogging away. I need to believe it was worth it.'

We are running some crappy formulas for life in these current generations. Times are changing for sure, each generation that comes makes modifications, learns from the ones before and makes their own mistakes. We'll get our heads around this nonsense soon enough. As pensions become less sure and mortgages become more expensive, at some point, popular opinion will swing the other way and there will be another reset.

But the truth is, philosophers, psychologists, teachers and leaders have been talking about 'purpose' for as long as we can remember. There's a reason for that. We are wired to look for meaning. As I wrote earlier in this book, I've met too many of you who know you are ignoring your calling to 'make a difference' (in whatever way that means for you) and I know from years of practice now that there's no need to collude in many of your stories that usually begin, 'you don't understand, it's different for me'. Sure, we all have our nuances, our circumstances, our upbringing, but you know, I'm going to keep saying it and saying it and saying it, *your biggest enemy is the voice in your head that holds you back.*

I'm not saying 'follow your passion', or 'if you build it, they will come', or 'you can make it in a year' or any of the trite surface comments that are being offered in the world as truisms. I'm saying that you are wired to look for meaning. And if you keep ignoring that tap on your soul, it is going to get louder until you take note. I promise you, it won't go away when you get the next car or the next holiday in the bag any more than it did last time you tried that.

Let's sit with what that might mean for a minute (because the other thing I see with many women who come into Remarkable Women is that they think I expect them to throw away all worldly things and step into the world ready to save it. (Frankly, the extremity of that thought seems to be key to enabling us to stay right where we are.) It's not a case of throwing all caution to the wind. I'm not asking you to throw your life in the air, sell everything and go work for a charity or solve world hunger. (OK, for some of you I am, because it actually is your thing, but it's less of you than you might think.) When it comes to Mission, *the Queen is constantly exploring ways to honour her talents and give them to the world.*

Stop for a minute and imagine a world where we all used our talents to the best of our ability. Where we abandoned the idea that we should play smaller, or spend our time pretending that we care about things that we don't care about at all (I'm going to be radical here, but I believe there are a hell of a lot less people who actually care about shareholder profit than pretend they do). Imagine a world where each of us looked at the thing we most long to see change in the world (more kindness, more equality, more love, more compassion, more connection, more community, more understanding and conversation, more fun, more adventure, more play – I can go on for a long time here…) and said, 'That one bit there feels really important to me, because I want more of it. What can I do to show up in service of *that* for the rest of my life?'

You see when we look around and sigh and say, 'I wish people would stop being so cruel to each other,' or 'I wish the leaders around here would realise we are all human beings,' or 'I wish someone would notice that we're all running around producing things in a really ineffective way,' we're just playing victim and we've lost sight of our Queen.

If you're sitting in an organisation and you can already see the one thing that you believe would make the biggest change (say it's as 'simple' as more kindness), YOU show up as the kindest person YOU can possibly be. Make it YOUR mission to practice kindness in deeper and deeper ways, to model it everywhere YOU go. The change starts with YOU.

Is that your lifetime mission? Possibly. Quite likely even. I guarantee that the more you give it your attention and intention, the more it will reveal itself. Whether it is or not, it's a powerful place to start. *Be the change you want to see in the world* as the famous saying goes. Be it. Make it your thing.

Queen Leaders don't have to run a charity, build a rocket or solve global education systems. They simply show up with the clear intention to be in Profound Service, however they define it. The rest unfolds from there.

Impact Over Ego – a Favourite Mantra

It's funny how many women wouldn't consider ego to be something that gets in the way. 'You must be kidding!' they laugh, 'I'm not one for shouting about what I do, I never push myself forward.'

And therein lies the problem.

Ego is about self-identity. *How you feel about yourself.* How you feel about yourself has a huge impact on how you show up in the world. In fact, I'd argue, it's the biggest limiting factor around. Yes, ego might have you appear cocky and brash, but if you don't identify with yourself as being the most brilliant person around here, or as having the irrepressible need to put yourself front and centre, it's more likely to be showing up in the ways you hold back.

It's your ego, your need to protect the form of self-identity that you have decided is important that might have you *not* speak up. It's your ego that may directly instruct you to play smaller, to stop chasing your dreams. It's one of the voices in your head that has you show up *contrary* to what feels most important to you, and it's why you often experience a split desire. Something like, 'I want to shine bright with all of my talents,' but also, 'I'd better not be seen as a show off, I want everyone to like me, so I'll dim down.' It's a conflict that's impossible to resolve.

When we sign up to a life of Profound Service, we acknowledge that we must not listen to the inner voice telling us to compromise what we know will be most impactful in order to protect a fabricated and unimportant self-image. We connect ourselves deeply to the impact we want to create, and every time the voice in our head invites us to tailor that in order to self-protect, we quietly whisper the mantra, 'Impact before Ego' to see what that allows us to choose instead.

Lightbulb Moment: Impact Over Ego in Real Life

My core talents are teaching and public speaking. I am extremely blessed in that I have no real experience of stage fright in the way that others articulate it. Yes, I get nervous, but the stage is my home. I love to be there and I have real confidence in shaping a loose framework and allowing my mind to create powerfully in the moment. I've been speaking in public since I was 12 years old (thinking I was prime minister in the making) and I grew up in a home where both of my parents were regularly speaking at the front of a room. To be honest, I thought it was just a thing everyone did. My real personal challenge when public speaking is that my ego has a brilliant way of dampening my message. You see, some of what I teach can sound a little odd to the uninitiated. (Imagine for a minute, getting up on stages in front of hundreds of people when the person before you has been talking about culture change or people engagement, with a speech entitled The Art of Queen Leadership. You kind of stand out from the crowd.) My ego wants to make it easy for the audience to get what I'm saying. In fact, no, that's not what my ego wants at all, my ego wants me to *make sure everyone likes me.* It also wants me to be seen as the best speaker of the day. I know. Not my proudest moment. Also, my truth.

You'd think that would have me show up really powerfully, right? Kind of. Also, no. In reality, it can dampen my impact significantly.

You see, if I focus my attention on having *everyone* in the room think I'm the best speaker on the stage, actually what happens is I moderate my message to make it easier for them to digest. Which means, the people who are really ready for this work don't get the full impact of it, they don't get me in Profound Service because I'm too busy looking at the bloke in the corner texting, and trying to get his attention back from his mobile phone.

In being something for everyone and responding to my ego's need to be liked and seen as the best, I give less service to those who really need me.

These days, if you were able to see inside my head before I get on stage, you'd see a thought-banner running constantly saying, 'Impact over ego, impact over ego, impact over ego.' In fact, these days, on the rare occasion there's a slide deck in play (because really, does the world need more PowerPoint?) you often see an opening slide that says 'Hustle' in big neon letters. That's my really edgy moment of any speech, because it's my choice to open with a key commitment.

'I can't be trusted to speak my full truth without this slide,' I explain to the audience, 'So while all the other slides are for you, this one's really for me. You see I really want you to like me and that gets in the way of what I have to say. At this point, I'm making a commitment that I will not be hustling for your approval today.'

My ego scans the room frantically to see if people think I am a little mad. Some definitely do – every time. But I'm all in now, because I've said it. There's no going back, so I continue doing everything I can to make sure that the people who are ready for what I have to say get the very best of what I have to give. That's me publicly declaring that I will choose my service to those of you who need what I have to say, before I let my ego drive the car to the top of the Public Speaking Popularity Charts.

This leads me neatly into this next concept that the Queen holds dear when it comes to Profound Service…

…Serving Not Pleasing

Sometimes, when I start to talk about Profound Service at conferences, I can literally see the faces screwing up. If we're in a more intimate setting, similar topics come up each time. I know what's coming, maybe you've already had the experience I'm about to describe. You see, there are a lot of women out there who've had enough of putting their needs to the back of the queue and self-sacrificing on every turn to ensure everyone else has what they need. I get it. And here's the good news, in case you've missed it in what I've shared so far, *that's not what Profound Service is all about.* Well, good news/bad news again of course. Especially for those of you who are hell bent on rejecting your own brilliance in favour of fitting in and pleasing.

The word 'profound' is really important here. I'm talking about deep, intense service that absolutely requires that your ego be put to one side AND that you stop pleasing. Because, believe it or not, all of that resentment about putting yourself last and everyone else first is *highly unlikely to match the definition of Profound Service*. If you're running around like a whirling dervish, doing all the things, juggling all the balls, making sure everyone has everything they could possibly need, then I put it to you that it's pretty much impossible for you to be doing anything profound at all.

I suspect strongly that what that creates in you is tiredness, resentment and sometimes anger. At the very least, an awareness that life feels distinctly out of balance. It's highly likely that you aren't doing a particularly great job of *anything* and that you're constantly waiting for people to notice what you've done and pat you on the back.

Does that sound like Profound Service to you?

No. Nor me.

When we sit with the idea that the Queen serves and does not please, we get to go a little deeper. We get to explore the ways in which we are going against our own inner wisdom, our great intuition. We hold up the mirror to the times we have been afraid to say, 'No' or to call out that the way a dynamic is working is out of alignment. We notice all the times we sigh inside and make a decision to 'suck things up' for the sake of harmony, or the group, or because we feel we should. If we pause long enough, we notice once again, that all of this could be different with a little courage. And a whole lot of Serving Not Pleasing.

You see, real service, Profound Service, requires the Queen to lean in and speak to the things no one else is speaking about. It requires us to be tuned into our inner wisdom and notice the times we actively dodge the conversation that needs to be spoken. It requires us to be willing to explore what it would take to have us show up and create something different. Our inner wisdom is the voice that's nudging us to be wholly honest and notice that for all our trying and pushing and exhausting ourselves, we are creating and re-creating the same situation over and over again.

Queen Work is so simple on one level. It requires that we be true to ourselves. And that we give what we most long to create to others with a clean, clear approach. Of course, sometimes simple feels like the hardest thing of all.

 ## Lightbulb Moment: Drop the Chameleon

I'm about to show my age here, and I'm guessing many of you will be familiar with the film Pretty Woman. It's about a millionaire (Richard Gere) who falls in love with a sex worker (Julia Roberts), who of course ends up teaching him just as much about life as he does her. I adored it as a teenager and suspect that even now, if I were to sit and watch it, I could recite most of the script. That said, having become more alert to the ways we romanticise certain behaviours in film and story that perpetuate the challenges of equality in the world, I confess this is a film I would struggle to watch now. No matter how nicely you wrap it up, it's a story with a problematic plotline as far as women are concerned.

Anyway, here's what you need to know. When Richard Gere meets Julia Roberts for the first time, asking for directions, he asks her what her name is. She responds, 'Whatever you want it to be.'

If there was ever a moment in a film that summed up a large chunk of my life, it's that line. When it dawned on me, it was a huge moment. You see, there are nuances to how 'pleasing' shows up in each of us. For many, it's obvious and crippling, for me it was more subtle. In fact, I'd argue, in many ways it was the key to how I smoothly moved up the career ladder from temporary secretary in a suburban construction firm to customer service director of one of the UK's largest companies.

I was a brilliant chameleon. In truth, I still am. From a very early age, I learned how to bring calm, humour or peace to a room. My volatile father had a habit of losing his rag at the smallest thing (imagine playing a board game with a 5-year-old and throwing the board in the air because you weren't winning), and it was clear to me that the whole family had an easier time when he was calm. I quickly learned to smooth things over, to empathise about the truly unfair nature of the dice he was throwing, to bring him cups of tea, to make him laugh. It became second nature to me.

I took this skill into my career, which began in a sub-contractor's office in the construction industry. The women were mainly in secretarial roles (me included), and whilst there was always plenty of banter, there was also a permanent sense of volatility when certain people were in the office. On more than one occasion that volatility led to fist fights. In that place, I honed my skills more. I learned to be 'one of the boys' whilst setting gentle boundaries on what was acceptable. I swiftly gained a reputation for being able to work with the most challenging men (a reputation that continued throughout most of my career). It became easy for me to move up the ranks in a world where I was able to bring something to the room that had people ease off and reconnect.

Let me also acknowledge, I was fairly smart and unafraid to speak up. I often had something to contribute – or at least I thought I did. It's important to say that because I see so many women walk past their natural talents. But I have no doubt in my mind that my ability to walk into a room and sense what was needed for cohesion and collaboration gave me a huge advantage. I was regularly 'serving', but the truth is it came with a real dollop of 'pleasing'. I would rarely stick my neck out for anything if I sensed it would lose me my place as 'the favoured one'.

I spoke my truth with a coating of, 'Is this what you need?'

It took me years to work out that I had lost a huge chunk of my sense of self in all of that. That I had overplayed my chameleon behaviour to such an extent that in many rooms, for all I would speak my case with groundedness and assertion, often I had lost sight of my own opinion. Instead, I would powerfully represent the opinion of my boss, mentor or sponsor so that I could go back and report like a 'good girl' who had met the requirements of her mission. I would regularly persuade myself to fall in line with their views, sometimes making adjustments to my values and principles accordingly.

If anyone is reading this book who knows me well, I'm guessing you might think I'm exaggerating here. Because let me be clear, I have always had strong Warrior tendencies and without knowing I was doing it, I had plenty of experience of being a Queen. *But it was always modified: there was always an element of 'pleasing' not 'serving'.*

This regularly showed up in me deferring to the most important person in the room, often speaking only to them when there might be ten others sitting at the table. (A smart boss of mine spotted this and badgered me about it for a long time. The truth is, I didn't see what the problem was.) My proposals were frequently designed to be what I thought the person I most wanted to impress wanted. I would choose carefully whose opinions mattered and work hard to keep them on side.

I can still remember the day it dawned on me that I had lost sight of my own opinion. That I had been 'pleasing' not 'serving' in a highly sophisticated way. That moment marked a pivotal change in my career, and later allowed my Queen to rise in her fullest glory. *I gave myself permission to discover who I was when I didn't care what anyone thought about me.*

From there, Profound Service was entirely possible. It was a liberating moment.

Take a moment. Explore how often and when you adjust the way you present yourself in order to please others. Note who the people are you're most inclined to do that with and what's going on in your head at the time. Especially, give attention to the times where you make tiny compromises to your values, beliefs and principles in order to please.

The Queen is human. She may find herself with these tendencies too. It's why she puts her attention on Profound Service and her mission in the world. Because when she serves a greater purpose, when she sees and believes in the possibility of what she can create, that need to be liked gets smaller – she knows she has more important things to do.

Chapter 9: Unlocking Your Mission

Like all things Queen related, a big juicy topic like 'Mission' takes time, which means it's important to start with this:

The Queen gives herself permission to evolve. She recognises growth takes time.

She knows that as her wisdom and experience increase, she will find more insights that will lead her to adjust and amend in many spaces. In fact, she knows that her ability to think again – once she has unlocked more information or tested out ideas – is deeply connected to her ability to grow and lead. She recognises that a fixed mindset with an inability to respond to what is occurring around her is a surefire path to trouble. She does not have it all sorted before she starts.

I know you'll be nodding sagely of course. This makes perfect sense. We can all name hundreds of examples in the real world of where an inability to flex has got organisations and individuals into trouble. It's easy to point the finger outward. Even the most self-aware of us will be able to find instances in our lives where we refused to see what was right in front of us. Developing an ability to create something that is fixed enough to give us focus, whilst having a degree of flexibility that allows us to change as circumstances change, or as we generate new information, is a significant skill.

We don't have it from day one.

So, when we sit down to explore what our mission might be in the world, it's daft to think we can nail it in an hour. And yet, that's what most of us seem to want. When we don't find it, it's tempting to think we should leave it alone, that 'Mission' isn't for us.

I want to hold you in the enquiry for longer. I want to show you how it evolved for me (and I suspect will continue to evolve). But before I do that, I want to pause again and share why I believe it's important groundwork to uncover what our mission is.

You see, so many of us are easily swayed by the less than trustworthy voice in our head that has us play small (although we repeatedly blame it on external circumstances or the behaviour of others). We all experience times in our lives where we make fear- and/or control-based decisions – those moments where our heart is calling us to do one thing and yet we literally turn our back on our inner wisdom and do something else. This is usually the 'safe' option as we define it in our heads, often the unappealing option, or at best, the modified option that is not even close to the vision we have in our minds.

When we lock onto a mission, albeit a loose North Star, and we cultivate our desire to introduce it to the world and see the impact it could create, we have a powerful way of turning away from the voice in our head, of choosing Impact over Ego. We have a way of saying 'No' for a greater 'Yes'. We enable ourselves to quieten the voice that says we are not good enough. We have a new route to showing up.

Mission is core groundwork for the Queen. When she has a strong sense of what she is here for, she has a path to follow, a sense of clarity that enables her to grow through her fears. Mission is a critical component to unlocking your truly remarkable uniqueness, to making the contribution you were designed to make in the world. Stay with it. Accept it will take time.

It took years for me. I'm still refining it. Yet, even with those adaptations, I see I'm still heading in a broadly similar direction, the same themes have always been my North Star. The focus simply becomes clearer. Whilst I don't know how to arrive and what arriving looks like, I definitely know what getting closer looks like. It's all about tiny steps.

Let me say more… In my experience, it's the real-life stories that help us all to understand ways these enquiries might unfold.

 ## Lightbulb Moment: Get on a Path to Reveal the Path

I landed the job of my dreams. I'd been secretly working towards it for years. Looking back, I question whether making it a secret was a good idea, but that's a different story. The reason why it was a secret was because I'd been informed in casual conversation by two former incumbents that I couldn't possibly even move to the department I had my eye on, because I didn't have the core skills and background and (somewhat bizarrely and irrelevant in my view), that my MBA didn't come from the 'right' university.

But I *did* get the job … only to discover that it wasn't what I had thought it would be. I did not fall in love with the work, and I struggled with the highly toxic political environment I found myself in, with peers who outright rejected me and were stuck in their own resentment about recent changes to our team structure. It was exhausting. All that work, those many years of attention and perseverance, to find this was not what I wanted at all.

I went to see my boss, a brilliant ex-army man who was used to big strategies and clever tactics. The poor fella was undoubtedly expecting a meeting where we did our usual – grabbed the pen for the flip chart and thought creatively together.

I leaned forward earnestly, enough was enough.

'I don't know what I'm on this planet for,' I said to the surprised face in front of me, 'but it's not this. I need to work it out fast or I'm going to have to leave.'

In an instant he turned his chair to his keyboard and began to type, which I found a little shocking, given my big revelation that seemed so important.

'What are you doing?' I asked, laughing nervously.

'I'm getting you a coach.'

Hallelujah for that moment, some eight or more years ago. It changed everything.

I started to probe around my purpose with my new confidante. At the beginning it was woolly and unclear. Something about releasing potential in others, allowing humans to see each other. Something about wanting to change the world. Nothing I could do anything with in any tangible sense, and yet it still felt like progress.

Looking back, my time with her was a clear Step One in a much longer process.

One year later I found myself on a plane to Spain, moving the enquiry up to the next level. Over the course of a year, I met with 14 other leaders from all over the world and we dug deep into our own questions when it came to leadership. I swiftly unlocked a Heart that had been protected for a long time in a desire to be 'successful' and 'professional', and with it came shockingly exciting results back at home. Suddenly and very unexpectedly, I found myself in a new job leading thousands of people. It felt like home, although I had never realised that was where I needed to be.

I talked a lot about creating an environment where everyone loved what they did and declared that it was my responsibility to make sure that happened. I could feel the change in me and the ripple effect in those around me almost every day. It was exciting. I wanted more. My work was purposeful and fulfilling.

Step Two was in full swing – I was on a mission to have people fall in love with what they did by unlocking new levels of potential.

And then, seemingly out of the blue, that job was also not enough, in the strangest and most unexpected way. I saw that I wanted to see what it was like to put *all of my attention* on allowing people to reveal their inner potential. I wanted to do it without the responsibility of representing a powerful well-known brand (which limited my freedom of speech and teaching), and I wanted to do it without having to worry about stakeholder return or KPIs. I didn't want to spend my precious time in a single conversation about how a widget fitted into another widget. (To be clear, I have the utmost respect for those who do, it's just not me and how my brain works.) Most surprisingly, I wanted to do this work with women. Having forged a strong reputation as someone who worked brilliantly with challenging men, I didn't see this one coming. And yet there it was. In many ways, it *does* make sense. I've always been a supporter of the 'underdog' and my heart has broken since a child whenever I have seen someone in a disadvantaged position. I'm a passionate believer in allowing people to stand on my shoulders when I see I can really make a difference, and I was now clear that I lived in a world where many brilliant women struggled to live into their brilliance and own their unique identity.

Step Three was to leave my huge corporate job and create a cleaner, purer Mission – one that I had complete autonomy over. It was time to start a business (it had a different name back then and now, of course, we know it as Remarkable Women).

I signed up to work with a world-leading coach. We were 18 months into the business, and though it was clearly going well for a newbie business in an industry we did not yet understand, things were not fast enough for me. For seven months, I met with a man I barely knew on Zoom to explore what I wanted to create. With him, I created a new mission statement, one that I agreed I would give myself 25 years to fulfil. For the first time, I entered into the idea that I could make this a fulfilling Long Game, rather than feeding myself with the adrenalin rush of trying to make everything happen today.

'I want 50,000 Heart-centred Leaders changing organisations from the inside. And a movement of remarkable women changing the world,' I declared, and continue to state when I'm teaching mission. This was Step Four in an evolving process that had taken eight years since I asked the original question. Always heading in a cohesive direction, getting clearer all the time.

There's more (I know!). Eventually Step Five made itself clear. The Mission above the Mission. Oddly enough, I don't have a thunderbolt moment that I remember vividly when I saw this, it was a softer, gentler knowing, coming from teaching topics like Zone of Genius (a concept originating from *The Big Leap* by Gay Hendricks) to women all over the world.

You see, one day I realised, that at the heart of all this, was something very simple.

I want to know who I am in my full potential.

It has taken me a long time to own that, and to indeed realise that me in my full potential means a lifetime of intention and attention, because, like you, *I am capable of so much more than I realise.*

I'm excited to dedicate my life to this and I'm committed to sharing what I learn with others. Even if it wasn't my business, I would be doing it. It's not something I 'have' to do, or believe I 'should' do, it's written on my bones. It's a mission that breathes inside of me.

Is this the end of the process of discovery of my mission? It would be daft to say yes, given it has now been a nine-year journey (and four and a half years into a 25-year-mission). New nuances are still revealing themselves to me. I'm on the path. It's a North Star that I cannot possibly know the full path to. What I do know is that I'm heading broadly in the 'right' direction and that today, I can't envisage a moment where I would close the door on the adventure. I love what it is creating. I want to keep going.

Chapter 10: The Long Game

'There are no impossible goals, only impossible deadlines.'
Brian Tracy

This mission thing takes time. All of this discovery takes time. Our need for instant gratification has us thinking that it should come quicker, and the very beauty of this life of Queen Leadership is that when the moment comes that we can lean into the idea that we can create tiny progressions every single day, the whole of life opens up to us in new ways.

You're not supposed to be able to answer 'what am I here to do?' at the end of a 90-minute masterclass, or even when you read this book. There is magic in uncovering the layers: testing, experimenting, trying on for size.

What you *are* supposed to do, in my humble opinion, is recognise that you are here to do *something.* The next step from there is to open your Heart and listen to all of those messages you keep offering to yourself in quiet moments and then putting down because they seem too jumbled, too scary, too hard. Sit with them, allow yourself time, get on *A Path* to reveal *The Bigger Path*.

The Queen is learning patience. She is wise.

She knows that she can make dramatic choices any time she likes, but that sometimes the choice is simpler: to head off in the direction that her instinct offers her, one single step at a time. She knows to remain committed to a single decision – to create impact with whatever it is she has chosen to do. She recognises that we often paralyse ourselves with fear of what might go wrong before we have done anything, and that the next simple step is rarely terrifying at all. She knows that for peace of mind she must respond to the whispers of her heart rather than try to squash them down.

And somewhere, in the midst of this wisdom, courage, faith and trust, something spectacular emerges. One day, the acorn shows it is clearly going to become a tree after all, and all of those small steps make perfect sense, even though we didn't think we were going fast enough at the time.

When I introduce women to the idea that the Queen is playing a Long Game, I can often visually see them mentally filing that idea in the 'not taking any notice' pile. It's literally like we can't compute. Our world has become so full of instant gratification and constant comparison that it's hard to get our heads around the joy of being in an Infinite Game, rather than one that needs to be won next week.

I get it. My Warrior is still strong. She's the one who wants to get everything done now. And believe me, I work at the speed of light – everyone who works closely with me sees it and comments on it (and that's in a life where I am consciously making an effort to slow down!). I understand the desire to do more, go faster and sometimes (far less often than you might think), that energy is well directed. There is a true need to take an immediate decision and move forward or to inject momentum when morale is dipping. Even in those circumstances, there is no justification for bringing Warrior behaviour to the mix. The way we BE in those moments counts. It's our role to generate excitement, enthusiasm, perhaps even a calm sense of capability. Choosing to ignite the battle cry instead has consequences.

If you have a strong Warrior inside you, then like me, you also know this, if you are willing to look deeply. *The Warrior goes fast at any cost.* Things get done with a sense of lightning speed that can verge on carelessness – a carelessness that misses what's really important in the big list of stuff. This carelessness removes humanity from circumstances and allows us to plough on at the cost of others, believing they are 'in the way' of something very important. It can cost us our own health (you're reading work by a woman who made daily choices that led her to spinal surgery and a period of three months of being unable to sit, let alone walk, I know this game), for some it will cost treasured relationships. There is always collateral damage when we subscribe to the idea that the end justifies the means.

When we allow ourselves to step into an Infinite Game, where there is only progress and more possibility, where there is no loser so that another can win, where there is no end in sight, we can relax into the idea that we are perpetually and constantly tapping into the glory of our potential. Can you imagine what you could really achieve if you were willing to give yourself a lifetime to do it? That's exactly what the Queen does. In the real world, her role is to rule her 'nation' with ease and grace until such point as there is no longer breath in her body. There is no 'win', there is only the possibility of growth, of expansion, of a deeper experience of life for her and those around her. It's an incredible metaphor for showing up in life.

You are capable of realising and creating so many things. Insisting that they all have to be done tomorrow, leaves two brilliant questions: *Did you enjoy creating them?* and *What are you going to do with yourself now all the things are done?* (And just in case you're living into that story that you're going to sit on a beach and drink cocktails all day for the rest of your life – *really?* Life without purpose or meaning is an interesting choice. History and centuries of learning present little evidence that we will find our bliss there.)

The Long Game isn't just for our overarching Mission either. It's how we show up every single day as leaders. You see, there are so many arbitrary deadlines in the world (some of which we've even set ourselves), that we've started to kid ourselves they are real. We sit in meetings and feel the tension flying through us at the idea that a project might go live a day or even a week late. We lose sight of what's important in getting swept up in the idea of getting things done NOW, and those of us with Warrior tendencies? – we're the worst of all.

Our ability to live in a Long Game is what keeps us strong, measured, balanced. Sure, it's fun to go fast, and whilst I've never been a huge fan of goals and objectives, even in my most structured corporate days, I can see they have value in motivating teams and in allowing people to unite around a common aspiration. Where they become dangerous is when we start to act as though they are immovable, inflexible, written in permanent marker, never to be changed. It is a core requirement that the Queen recognises the brilliance of the Long Game, the one where everyone wins and where we all stop trading short-term wins for long-term damage. It is the role of the Queen to remember that *it is all a game*, so that she can discern between what matters and what doesn't.

I see time and time again that most of us couldn't actually care less about shareholder profit. It doesn't matter to many in any way whatsoever that the thing we have scheduled for 10am on Monday is completed at 10am. But, wow, have we created and lived into systems that make us believe we do care!

The Queen does not rush towards arbitrary timelines, especially when she sees people are being damaged in the process. In the game where everyone is enrolled in the pleasure of playing and growing, her eye is on a bigger prize. Her decision making comes from that place. She knows that *most things make no difference at all*.

Lightbulb Moment: What Really Matters

Before we go any further, I want to sit with a thing I often get challenged on at conferences and major speaking events and even when I put articles out into the world.

This idea that we have somehow trained ourselves to think we care about things we don't care about – it's a biggie. There are a lot of people who don't like it much when I bring it up – especially senior leaders who build their corporate messaging on the idea that they absolutely can persuade people to care about things that don't really matter much at all. I did it myself for a very long time.

You see, most of us haven't noticed it in ourselves either. Honestly, the only time I have ever really cared about share prices is when I personally had enough shares in that organisation for it to make a significant difference to MY LIFE (that's why companies give out shares to senior leaders by the way), but it didn't matter a hoot to most of my people. In fact, I suspect if they had known just how many shares I had, they would have been even less inclined to create a return for me that they had no share of.

Most of us don't really care that much about profit at all. We can be lured into creating results through a sense of achievement or competition (often with some pretty terrible and patronising 'prizes') or by feeding our need for validation or belonging.

Most of the tactics used to get us hooked on those games are manipulation. I don't necessarily think it's cold-hearted manipulation (although of course, there are plenty of organisations who really don't care at all about their people), but it's still manipulation. Even when we attempt to connect people to meaning and purpose, we can do a fairly shoddy job of it, often because we are layering meaning onto something else entirely. It's 'froth' on the coffee and people can smell it a mile off. If we can't get people to care about something we've made up, we need to look at what it is we've created and go again, rather than think they're just not smart or invested. Why should anyone be truly invested in something that is smoke and mirrors, no matter how well we dress it up?

Then there's a challenge that arises even when we do notice that we don't care. Because the next thing we see, is that no one else is talking about it (or that it's a bit of a covert conversation that we're supposed to pretend we're not having) and so we stay quiet and carry on with the madness. We do what it takes to fit in.

I happen to believe we can create results *and* stop pretending. In fact, I think we create far more effective results by turning our attention to the things we *really* care about and connecting them into our day-to-day lives as leaders.

Many of us are living a life in the Western World that we often describe at Remarkable Women as being sucked into 'The Vortex'. We've been born into a world that has us chasing more: more money, more status symbols, more recognition, more validation. You know this. I know you do. Yet, like I said in my first book, *Remarkably Easy*, knowing it doesn't mean we're as savvy as we think we are. Knowing something isn't usually enough to have us chart a different course. Yet sometimes, something comes along that has us click and make a change. Maybe now will be that time for you.

You do not need more of what doesn't make a difference. You do not need to comply and conform to rules and systems that literally hook you like an addict onto rewards that neither feed nor nourish you.

I'm not suggesting you give everything up and live a life of simplicity (although if that's for you, then go make it happen). I am passionate about an awakening that allows us to change the systems, that allows our impact to be truly meaningful. To do that requires a willingness to let go and experiment with what could be possible then.

The Queen knows the formulas for success in the modern world are pretty shoddy. She knows that more things, more titles, more pats on the back *do not equate to finding peace with our lives.* The Queen is longing to make a difference. I'll keep saying it, it's easier than you think – *you can do more than you can imagine.*

Getting started requires opening our eyes and noticing that we have taken a few funny turns along this path of life and bought into some beliefs that are simply not true. From there, we make new choices.

Sweating the Small Stuff

We'll be coming back to the idea of discernment later in the book, but it really starts in Profound Service – in the realisation that we cannot do a*ll the things* and that it is not wise to attempt to. That if we truly intend to show up in the world with *profound* service, we must be discerning about where our attention and our energy goes. This is core to how we make a difference.

On one level of course, we absolutely know this. And yet, our Warrior can be strong with this one. Fundamentally, she tends to have an underlying belief that she can do *all the things*, even when her body tells her no. She has a funny old habit of working until she falls over and then recovering either on holiday or sometimes, when she's really pushed her luck, in hospital.

We all need to drop the trivia. For some of us that's battling over every small thing that comes our way in our professional life, and for others it's our perfectionism which makes us believe that things that don't even really matter have to be just so. It's attention to this trivia that gets in the way of us truly making a difference with ease and grace.

The Warrior will go to battle on pretty much anything. She tenses up when she senses something is wrong and her radar is a little shoddy when it comes to what's worth the fight and what isn't. Of course she fights – battle is her thing. When something comes up that looks like it needs a spot of justice, determination and getting things done, she'll stand to attention, ready to make her move. She'll fight for the Christmas party budget just as willingly as she'll go to war for world peace. She has very little discernment because she relies on reaction to drive action.

The Queen has no desire to be in battle. Why? Because battles drain energy. They leave a mess behind that needs clearing up (which rarely happens and then the chaos truly unfolds) and they create pain and division. Battles hurt people. They leave long-term damage.

Instead of going to battle, the Queen chooses wisely what gets her energy and what doesn't. She recognises that some of the battles she would have previously entered so readily are actually a way of keeping her away from the things that really matter. She applies discernment in a way that the Warrior simply cannot.

It's easy to be distracted by trivia. A main factor in our constant 'busy-ness' is our inability to discern what matters and what doesn't. Those of us who work fast, believe we just need to go faster and get even more done, without checking to see what's important and what isn't, while those of us who are slower and more reflective can find themselves going round in circles perfecting things that are long past their useful date.

The Queen doesn't sweat the small stuff. She knows she needs to be alert to potential distractions at all times – the temptation of more, the battle that will not change anything, the noise in her head that tells her she's not enough. All of these things keep her away from doing the things that matter most. Discernment is one of her strongest skills. In order to make it strong, she practises it every single opportunity she can. She asks pertinent questions, like: *Does this really make a difference? Is this good use of my limited supply of energy? What would happen if I didn't do this at all?*

War vs Surrender – It's More Nuanced than That

As we draw this section on Profound Service to a close, it's important to offer a clear distinction. Whilst the Queen does not run rampage, declaring war and starting battles wherever she goes, she also does not roll over, surrender and play 'nice'. When we teach Queen, we often have women coming proudly to us, declaring that they have found a way to accept things that are clearly in conflict with their values or the things they want to create in the world. Over time we've realised that we've been creating that impression ourselves (of course we have) by forgetting to talk about what happens when someone declares war on the Queen or her people, or indeed when something occurs that is dramatically conflicting with our values – something that every bone in our body suggests we cannot and should not be silent about.

Let's start with the war scenario. It's highly likely that at some point, the Queen will find herself face to face with someone who wants to fight to the death and who is willing to introduce all kinds of measures to make that happen (in organisational life that may show itself as outright bullying or often more subtle coercive 'land grabs' – those times where someone is making underhand moves to assert their position and reduce yours at the same time). What to do then? The answer is straightforward: *Remain in integrity with who you are and what you stand for.*

A real Queen would not roll over and surrender her nation, or indeed find a way to agree to something that was not a match to her Mission and her truth. Crucially, she would not play dirty. She would neither seek revenge nor justify actions from herself that she would never tolerate in others. She does not believe the ends justify the means. She takes a clear stand for her people, her legacy, her own integrity. She knows she must be able to look herself in the eye when this is all over and feel deeply proud of her actions rather than need to find a way to make them seem acceptable.

'War' scenarios are complex. They are challenging to navigate. Our Warrior will rise to fight quickly and valiantly for what is 'right'. It's easy to listen to the voice in our head that loses sight of our own accountability and simply seeks to exact justice on those around us. The answers of what to do are unlikely to be obvious. How you show up is crystal clear. We do not seek to cause pain or retribution, and if war is declared, we take our position in it considerately, always remembering that real humans are involved, even when we do not agree with them or even like them. The Queen goes to War with a Heart at Peace. Whatever the outcome, she wants to recognise herself, her humanity and the humanity of others throughout.

Am I saying this guarantees you a 'win'? Of course not. I'm not saying any Queen move guarantees you a win. If I had the skill to teach you certainty of outcome in every scenario, I'd be God rather than a woman leaning into another woman, sharing what she knows. I am saying that at the end of any extreme scenario, whatever the outcome, the Queen wants to be able to look at herself in the mirror and say, 'I did my very best'. For the Queen leader, that means standing up for what she believes in AND maintaining her integrity.

Disarming the Warrior

It's also important to talk about how the Queen operates in a world full of Warriors (you and me included). It's really quite common for women to come to me, sigh and say, 'Yes, but Danielle,' (I always know this is going to be a good one when you start that way) 'the only thing these Warriors respond to is my Warrior. I need to bring it, even if I lose. I have to do the right thing.'

As we move into the next section, our deep exploration of Ruthless Compassion and what it means to show up with our truth, I hope that you will begin to see there is another, far more powerful way to engage, *even and especially with the Warriors.* And I get it. Some of these energies are difficult to manage. It can feel hopeless.

The thing I want to remind you of is that if you insist on bringing Warrior to a situation where there is strong Warrior behaviour at play, you'd better be the strongest in the room. Because it will never be a battle of 'right' and 'wrong', it will be a battle of strength. They are simply not the same thing. If you believe that facts and logic will disarm a Warrior you will be mistaken – after all, they don't disarm YOU. They don't have you believe that you are wrong after all. You simply dig in harder. Knowing that this is the automatic response of any leader in Warrior mindset, in service of finding a smoother route through that does less or even no damage, bringing in Queen is imperative.

Where do we start? Looking at ourselves of course. *How am I creating this?* is a critical question once again.

You see, so many women out there think that their 'adversary' is unreasonable, irrational, manipulative, deceptive and fundamentally has some kind of character flaw that justifies battle. What I'd like to show you now, and what the Queen always owns, is that we *all* have these traits in us to some degree. The difference between you and the

Warrior currently making your life hard, is almost certainly that they are simply being a little more honest about it than you.

Don't know what I mean? Well, let's take this next scenario, one that I come across regularly. You sit across from me at a table and you explain how you are 'doing the right thing' and that they are 'in it for themselves'. You usually follow that with how reasonable you have been and how they are not responding to your 'nice' requests to meet and to talk things through.

This is the point where I usually get out the bullshit button. You see, there is an enormous difference between 'saying the right things' and 'being' or 'enacting' the words you are speaking. We can all smell inauthenticity a mile off. If your deepest desire really is that someone, lord knows who, just hurries up and gets this person fired, do you really think that they can't *smell* that on you, no matter how nice your words are? Do you really think you aren't simply in a battle of wills where you BOTH want to eliminate the other?

Just because you *say it nicely*, doesn't mean you *mean it*.

How does the Queen disarm the Warrior? She shows up with her truth. It might be as scarily honest as saying, 'I think we're in a battle to the death here, aren't we? Are you open to trying something different or is that our chosen route?' (*Tone really matters here,* because this is an open conversation, not a threat). Or even, 'You know, I have this sense that we don't like each other much. I'm a bit exhausted with it. What would it look like to create a relationship where we're at least not sabotaging each other?'

Bold stuff, I know. And... it starts with you. Where are you being dishonest in this relationship? Where are you manipulating? Where are you hoping fake niceness will win

81

the day? Bring Queen. Bring Ruthless Compassion. Speak your truth with clarity, kindness and positive intent. Stop bullshitting yourself.

Standing Up for the Truth

So how do we stand up for the truth then? And when 'should' we back off? There are a million scenarios we could play with here, and many writers and thinkers more talented than me have created approaches for the complex issues we face in everyday life, in leadership and when it comes to global challenges. Part of evolving into a stronger Queen is experimentation, practice, muscle strengthening and uncovering what works for you.

As we move into the next section and explore what it means to practise Ruthless Compassion, we'll go deeper into how the Queen chooses to look in the eyes of interpersonal, group and wider organisational conflict, but for now let me borrow from Brené Brown, who puts it perfectly:

'Daring leaders who live into their values are never silent about hard things.'

You may not feel that you are clear on your values, and this is simpler than you think. Stop for a moment and listen to the wise soft voice inside you. You will know your real truth, underneath the noise and justification. We always do.

The Queen does not live in a bubble. She is clear about who she is and what she believes in. She is not the 'neutral' person in the room. She assesses situations against her values and her Mission and she considers her position carefully so that she can take powerful action. She is willing to go deeper into her own emotion, her own beliefs and her own assumptions in order to create a lasting impact on an issue. Once again, she recognises that this is a Long Game and she is unlikely to change fixed positions in a single conversation. She takes stock and draws in her Wisdom Council.

She stands back in order to move forward.

Our Warrior has a tendency to launch straight in – to speak whatever comes to her mind in a hot-headed moment. Her anger is misunderstood (even by her) and left to rampage around a room with little consideration of who becomes collateral damage in service of getting to the immediate outcome – submission of the enemy. Our inner Warriors easily find a way for the ends to justify the means.

It doesn't take much for any of us to see why the results the Warrior creates may have us feel better and proud in the moment, but still leave us with an aftertaste that shows the result is nothing like as effective as we imagined. We can see the impact of this way of winning all over the world. It's the very thing most of us long to change, even though we may not articulate it that way. We cannot change anything with the same behaviour that created it in the first place. What we continually do is simply reverse the balance of power, create resentment somewhere else, that eventually rises and does damage and engenders a new battle. Our need for instant results and our justification for riding roughshod over others, gets us into trouble in the long run – if not individually, then for sure as a human race.

The Queen is wiser. She wants more for the world. She is clear what she stands for and she takes a stand for it. She is not seeking to win the battle. Her deepest desire is to end the war in a meaningful and lasting way. One of the ways in which she learns to do this, is cultivating the muscle of Ruthless Compassion. It's time to go there next.

Before we do, stop for a moment. Breathe. We've covered a lot. Some of it may feel edgy. Sit with your thoughts. Give yourself permission to start small. Remember, it's a Long and Exciting Game.

CORE FOUNDATION TWO:
RUTHLESS COMPASSION

Chapter 11: What is Ruthless Compassion?

This next section is where we dig in deep. I truly believe that at the heart of almost every human problem in the world is a failed human interaction: key moments where we have failed to address a growing conflict dynamic, or where we have tried, but come up miserably short. Our inability to address the 'elephant in the room' shows up everywhere. The repercussions are wide ranging and damaging. In our families, friendships, communities and organisations. Queen leaders know that the muscle of Ruthless Compassion is one that they must cultivate every single day, regardless of the moments they may get it wrong, or even fall flat on their faces. They understand it is an essential part of their growth and the impact they create.

Like Yin and Yang, when it comes to Ruthless Compassion, we find two words that are almost in opposition to each other. How can you be both ruthless *and* compassionate? Brutal and loving. Yet at the point at which we find supreme balance between the two words, something magical happens: *We finally find ourselves able to say the things that hardly anyone can say, with the love and compassion that enables others to receive them.*

If I was speaking this aloud, I'd pause, breathe in and out and say the sentence again, so that you would realise it is a collection of words that is not to be skimmed over swiftly. Stop for a minute, read it again, take in what it means.

In my professional career, if I was paid even a penny for every conversation we had about why 'people' couldn't have 'difficult' conversations, I'd be a very rich woman by now. I engaged in those chats vigorously and foolishly more times than I can remember. Eventually, I came to a simple truth:

How can we expect others to be good at it, when we are not good at it ourselves?

My work has always had an underlying theme that speaks to making things easy. It regularly struck me as madness that we were inviting people to attend courses to learn how to speak 'difficult' things. And yet, what we were asking *was* difficult, and the processes that were so carefully designed to make it easier weren't helping at all. They seemed to miss the inevitable fact that the other person in the conversation hadn't been trained in the process and therefore had no intention of following it. These conversations were repeatedly unpredictable, painful, regularly disastrous and frequently avoided like the plague. This cycle shows up in almost every place where there is human interaction.

At the heart of all that was the truth of my own challenge when this particular problem emerged for me. I had a great sense of what everyone else was up to, because I was doing it too. I'd turn a blind eye to all kinds of things in my life, hoping against hope that they would somehow improve themselves. My perpetual desire to avoid conflict and keep things harmonious would have me pretend things weren't happening in favour of dodging the 'difficult' conversation I'd need to have in order to resolve it. When, finally, circumstances conspired (as they always did and do) and I found myself with little choice but to dive in and attempt to resolve the situation, I'd spend hours at night playing and replaying conversations in my head in rehearsal of what was to come. My stomach would be full of anxious butterflies for hours beforehand and I'd enter the conversation with a heavy heart, dreading the pain I was sure would ensue. It was a recipe for disaster.

As I moved swiftly up the ranks of my organisation, I realised I needed to find another way – not least for my own sanity. As I looked around the organisation I found two clear personalities when faced with 'difficult' conversations. Both were creating havoc.

The first was *the Brutal Robot*. Seemingly uncaring, this person would open a conversation, say what had to be said, barely looking the other person in the eye and summarily laying out consequences with no option or opening for discussion. They were 'in and out fast' kind of people, avoiding future conversations by playing the 'busy' card and generally exuding an air of 'don't care' (it took me a while to realise there was more to it than that on the inside). They were firm, closed, swift, ruthless. When people cried in pain or frustration, they closed down more, believing their clarity would end the situation, even if others didn't like the outcome. Funnily enough, as a technique it was rarely successful. At least, not if you consider a success factor to be the avoidance of a messy trail of toxicity and resentment that created further problems in the future.

The second group? These were *the Caring Ones*. So keen not to hurt the person in front of them, they'd dance around the issue with wide sympathetic eyes, softening the message so that it could barely be heard, careful not to set off any land mines, continuing to pretend that the problem was not as big as it clearly was. They'd deliver the traditional 'shit sandwich' (as it's known in human resources circles) with lots of bread and butter and hardly any of the smelly bit. This left the people they had spoken to with no idea of the seriousness of the problem and a trail of messy incomplete process behind them that was ripe for bigger complaints about their leadership and handling of the matter in future.

In the first group, there was way too much ruthlessness, while in the second, misguided and ineffective compassion. Yet, somewhere in the middle, it was clear to me there must be a sweet spot. *How could we say the things that needed to be said in a way that would allow them to be heard and acknowledged, whilst still maintaining love, care and humanity for the person in front of us?*

A Balanced Path

There are other phrases out there that speak to this. Often when we teach Ruthless Compassion, we hear people talk excitedly about the excellent *Radical Candour* by Kim Scott, and the equally great, *Fierce Conversations* by Susan Scott (must be something in that surname!). I would definitely say 'Yes' to both of these resources for exploring more, *but* there's something exquisite about the idea of Ruthless Compassion. It allows us to do that thing that most of us are deeply longing to experience – *love* the person sitting in front of us *and* say the things that matter. It's that potent combination that makes all the difference.

It's no surprise then that I can't claim credit for this phrase and that in fact, it is rooted in the incredible world of meditation mastery that my brilliant business partner and modern-day monk, Nic (also known as Mahita) is a part of. This concept is as old as time. You see, one of the things we have seen in our work over the last six years together (and far longer as friends and colleagues) is the enormous possibility that opens when we put our attention on the Yin and the Yang in the world – the light *and* the darkness, the Doing *and* the Being. The difficult *and* the easy. There is a sweet spot when so many of these opposites come together that creates utter magic.

It's the same for Ruthless Compassion. It takes away the requirement for 'difficult' conversations and replaces them with loving, truthful ones. Allowing us to show up with what is really present for us, whilst truly seeing a real human being in front of us – another person that has the same human right as us, to exist, belong, love and be loved, and thrive. In these conversations, there is infinite potential to shift everything.

Of course, like all elements of Queen, Ruthless Compassion is a muscle we need to build. Most of us come to the practice with legacy around fear of conflict, or history of being too much, or scars of where these circumstances have not gone so well in the past. Most of us have tendencies to lash out at those we love in frustration and inability to express ourselves, and to avoid, avoid, avoid whenever we see a problem looming. It's a human condition. There are many who pretend it doesn't exist for them, and yet all you need to do is look into the relationships around you and you'll see it everywhere. We're all dodging the 'elephant in the room' at some point in time. In families, in organisations, in communities, in societies.

When the Queen learns to address what others are ignoring, she creates impact that is far beyond that which most of us can even imagine. Ruthless Compassion is her Superpower. Best of all, it doesn't work without love and compassion, so we never get to manipulate it to our own ends. We can all spot a false conversation a mile off. You cannot fake this one.

The good news is, there is a framework we can follow in order to practise, although as with all things impactful, it's not a cut-and-paste job. This is a way of *Being*, not a tactic. Much of the work is internal, rather than the conversation itself. Isn't it always?

I'm excited to show you what we've learned. In these next pages, you get to unlock something spectacular that will absolutely change your life, if you're willing to play.
Are you?

It Starts Here

Good news/bad news as we say around here, and it should be no surprise by now: the art of Ruthless Compassion starts with YOU. You see, a fundamental reason why we mess up in the conversations that really count is because our ego is in the way, *big time.*

Once again, it's not that side of the ego that is pushing itself forward (although of course, that can be an issue when we are absolutely certain we're in the right about something and we'll come to that shortly), it's the side that knows the conversation needs to be had, but that absolutely doesn't want to be the one to deliver it.

We adopt many strategies to take away the pain that *we* are experiencing. In our heads, it can often become all about not wanting to hurt the other person. Even though we know that the conversation needs to happen, we really wish someone else would take it on. We have to get clear of our own stuff long before we initiate the conversation with someone else. Otherwise, in reality, whatever comes out of our mouth is really about us: making sure we're not the villain, or being the villain (and knowing it), and trying to escape as soon as possible so that we don't see the damage we've done. We're trying to keep the pain away from us when it shouldn't be about us at all. Profound Service means that we sit with all of our own noise and use the resources we have to process them so that our own issues have as little impact on the conversation as possible. We focus on Impact before Ego.

 Lightbulb Moment: What's Really True Here?

I was sitting in a room with eight colleagues and my boss. As often happened in this organisation that I loved, but occasionally deeply hated, I found myself in a meeting talking about resource cuts.

I detested these conversations. The truth is we were a highly successful business, creating shareholder returns that most organisations would only dream of. And yet, every year, without fail, we'd get the dreaded message, 'Make the cuts, we've got too fat.'

There was truth in that for sure. Somehow, we had created this Perfect System that in my eyes was failing us horribly. We'd rein back each year, working through all of the places where we could find efficiencies, and then later in the year, we'd all get to arguing our case for bringing more people back, only to find ourselves in the same position. Too many people, too many overheads.

We were all part of the problem and not one of us had come up with a smarter way forward. Which meant that each year, fight it though we might, at some point we'd get a very clear GET ON WITH IT instruction and then we'd succumb like little sheeples to the task in front of us, not wanting to be seen as the person who didn't have the metal to be one of the most senior leaders. This is what we got paid the big bucks for after all. So, after protesting loudly and getting precisely nowhere, we'd sit in meetings, working through our plans. Bitter and resentful on the one hand, whilst on the other, showing our best face and making it clear we were totally up to the job. Gossiping and colluding outside the meeting, but in it, doing the 'right thing' to protect our *very* well-paid backsides.

This particular day, I had at least had the sense to send my Warrior on a coffee break. Every time I had brought her into these conversations, like everyone else who had tried, I had been told in no uncertain terms to toe the line. It was a failing strategy. I tried a different way and leaned forward mid-conversation, 'I'm tired of pretending this isn't hard and it doesn't hurt,' I said. 'I'm tired of us all sitting in this meeting never acknowledging that we hate this and pretending we all find it easy. Can we at least find some space to process how we feel so that we don't take that energy into the conversations we're about to have?'

To my surprise (because at this point, I had no idea if anyone would back me or not), the conversation took an immediate turn. Suddenly, it became OK to say, 'I feel that way too'. The next week, my boss put aside half a day to sit together and talk through the conversations we were dreading and to coach each other on better ways to show up for them.

Is this the perfect ending to the story? Of course not. I was still learning. I'm a smarter Queen now than I was back then. Do I think the actual lay-offs were the right thing to do? No, to be honest. I still believe we let people down and that there is a better way than constant restructuring. In fact, let me be clearer. I still believe I let people down. I can't change that, but I can do better now I know better.

What I do know is that day we made real progress in honouring how we felt and I know that half-day meeting meant that the way we had those conversations was entirely different than it would have been had we all carried on pretending it simply didn't hurt. For that, I'm supremely grateful.

Chapter 12: Getting Clear of Your Stuff

This is a non-negotiable stage in the process of Ruthless Compassion. In order to truly show up with powerful impact for the other person, sitting down beforehand and getting clear on where you are struggling is critical. It's very different to 'rehearsing' how the conversation is going to go (which is what most of us do in these circumstances and is frankly, pretty pointless, because we cannot possibly predict how the other person will respond to even our opening sentence) and requires us to be honest.

In fact, it takes us back to the primary question of the Queen: *How did I create this?*

I'm grateful we get to return to that question so many times in the course of this book. It's a tricky one and one that the Queen commits herself to mastering in service of her own growth and impact.

Let me remind you again of three key factors in this question (because they are easy to forget):

- This is not a finger-pointing exercise. The question is not, 'In what ways is this my fault?' and an opportunity for self-attack and flagellation. It is an honest enquiry into our part in the situation.
- There can be no question that you absolutely DO have a part to play in the creation of your current circumstances. The more honest you can be about that in service of the outcome you are consciously creating, the better.
- The question does not suggest that the other person does not have a part to play in current circumstances too. Of course, they do. What the question is allowing

you to do is turn your influence and attention to those things that you have the direct opportunity to change – your own thoughts and actions.

Our natural tendency is to look outwards and into the face of what another person or group has done or is doing wrong. In doing so, we brilliantly deflect from our own part. One of our favourite resources at Remarkable Women for exploring the essence of conflict is *The Anatomy of Peace* by the Arbinger Institute (it's a very easy read and not the academic tome that the title might suggest). The model in the book asks us to notice that once we have decided the other person is in the wrong (or indeed, once we have realised we are going to need to do something to them that is in conflict with our own values), we immediately set about inflating in our minds all the things that make that person very wrong indeed, whilst at the same time inflating our own goodness and virtue. We need to do that in order to 'harden our Heart' towards them and to give ourself permission to do something that we inherently sense is not the best course of action. In psychology, it's known as Cognitive Dissonance. When we choose to do something that some part of us knows isn't aligned to our core beliefs, we usually don't change our thinking, we justify our actions instead.

Ruthless Compassion invites us to *open our Heart* in service of creating a powerful conversation and ultimately, a powerful outcome for everyone concerned. That means we must watch for the trap of inflating the 'badness' of others and the 'goodness' of ourselves. Understanding how we are feeling and what our role has been in getting to this place, is one of the foundational keys to creating a very different kind of conversation. We've all been in the other kind. They don't tend to go so well. So, how do we get 'clear' of our stuff? We create space to sit with it. In my experience, it's useful to do it alone first, and then to share with a wise colleague or friend later (we'll come to how to select those individuals shortly, because that's a key place of discernment!).

I highly recommend a pen and paper and use of the 'SFD' technique, as coined by author Anne Lamott in outlining her process for aspiring authors, and later expanded on by Brené Brown for the purposes of 'rumbling' with our story.

The SFD Process

SFD stands for 'Shitty First Draft'. It's a simple concept, requiring a pen, a piece of paper and some space without distraction. That piece of paper is your place to run wild, to express how you are feeling at the most basic level. To say the things that are flowing through you with no need to edit or worry about what the reaction of others might be. You get to destroy it when you've finished. No-one is going to read it.

Why do it then?

As adults, there are very few, if any places where it's OK for us to speak our truth without editing. We're constantly adapting for our audience and how they might perceive us. Worrying about whether we sound childish, too much, too pathetic, not strong enough, not capable enough, unreasonable, petulant, the list goes on…

What seems to happen as a consequence of editing our very real thoughts and holding them inside, is that our mind starts to churn things around internally, like a broken record, surfacing them again and again. Something happens when we put these thoughts on paper, it's as though they feel heard. They often soften as a consequence. In fact, Brené Brown is very clear in her research that shame, a classic emotion when we are working with our own 'stuff', cannot survive being spoken.

Here's the trick though – watch out for when you edit *even though no one is watching.* It's always fascinating to me when I use the SFD technique (and I use it often) to find my pen hovering in mid-air as I mentally attempt to rephrase this document that no one is ever going to read. What I see is there are emotions and feelings I don't even want to own to myself. These are the very statements that need to come out most. Knowing they are unreasonable or childish.

Keep writing until there is nothing left to say. (Truly nothing. That's different to the voice in your head telling you that you must have finished by now.) The process is cathartic, brutally honest, liberating and regularly allows you to see a different perspective, at the very least unburdening a tiny part of the load you are about to carry into the conversation.

I often find an SFD offers me relief for an hour or two when the situation is particularly challenging for my mind to handle. What do I do when the noise starts to resurface (which it often does)? I go again, picking up my pen and paper and expressing what is now front of mind. This is a technique that never runs out. Use it until you don't need it anymore.

An important note about the SFD

If you're anything like me, a 'very busy and important person', there may be a voice in your head saying, *I'll just skip this bit* or *I'll pretend I've written it, but really I'll just say it in my head. It's not like she'll ever know and it'll pretty much do the same job, I bet.*

Nice try. Good luck with that.

This is a conversation that some part of you is dreading. The very fact that your mind is churning through what's going to happen and rehearsing options or justifying the things you believe you're about to say is a clear sign that you're not ready for the conversation – that you'll fudge it, avoid it or make a total hash of it. Getting clear of your stuff is critical if you are to truly show up with impact.

Do the work, so that you can finally learn to have a different kind of conversation: one that sees the human in front of you and that changes the dynamic into something that now has possibility.

It's a new kind of rehearsal – one that has you strip off a layer of anxiety or anger and that allows space for something new to emerge.

A Wise Ear

When we're grappling with Ruthless Compassion, it often helps to have a place where we can be truly honest. A conversation with someone who will call us out and refuse to collude in our stories – someone who is unattached to the outcome and full of powerful questions to help us explore. The Queen knows that who she chooses to confide in is critical and she is wise enough to realise there is never any need to go it alone.

If we really want to make progress in building our Ruthless Compassion muscle, we need to watch for the old tricks that will show up in both the Victim *and* the Warrior mindset. You see, both the fighter in us and the Victim will look for people to share with who will back us in our thinking. Perhaps we think it's unfair that we 'have to' have this conversation when 'they' should have dealt with it. Maybe we want to get stuck in and gossip about the faults of the other party or individual in order to feel better about the conversation we're about to initiate. These things are unhelpful when we commit to Ruthless Compassion. They serve to inflate our own position and 'rightness'. These are the conversations where it can be hard to say, 'I know this needs to happen, but, wow, it hurts – how can I sleep at night knowing I might do damage to another human being?'

Somehow, when we share with others, we can find ourselves showing up with a veneer of inauthenticity, of justification, of bravado. When we choose people who collude, or who have a tendency to step in and 'fix' us we get nowhere. Likewise, with those who invalidate our feelings with the kind of useless advice that says, 'You just need to stop feeling like that, it's not helping.' These are not our 'Go-to People' when we need to step into something that in truth, we would do anything to avoid.

Instead, we search for the individual who will hold us to something bigger than our neurosis or self-justification. We look for someone who will point lovingly to the clues in our tone of phrase that suggest we are blaming or refusing to own our part in the situation in which we find ourselves. We talk to the person who allows us to exist within our messy feelings and poke around with raw honesty, in service of creating a new way forward. They are the people who encourage us to shoot for 'The High Dream'. Choose wisely who you share with. And then share from the Heart.

 ## Lightbulb Moment: The High Dream

I found myself in yet another restructuring scenario (the lessons from such situations feel like another book in themselves). This time, thousands of people's lives and living patterns were affected. The decision to create the change felt solid this time, albeit edgy and difficult. It really did feel like the 'right' thing to do in order to get us out of a longstanding, messy problem that we had created many years earlier (the fact that we had taken so long to do it had for sure exacerbated the issue we now faced and yet, here we were, ready to change).

I knew I was the right person to lead the conversation. I'd been building my skills in Ruthless Compassion for a long time. It needed to be me and I wanted to show up as powerfully and compassionately as I could.

I also knew that there was an incredibly high potential that I was in for many sleepless nights and that the lack of sleep itself and the anxiety that would accompany it could easily throw me off balance, and lead to poor decisions and downward spirals. Real livelihoods and ways of living were on the table here and they were precious to me. Deep down, my ego had stuff to say too. I had a fear of becoming the villain and indeed, of making a mess of this. There was a bigger picture of the impact on others and also, the egocentric position of the impact on me and my reputation. I wanted to be known as the leader who really saw and understood people and who demonstrated another way, but I knew from history that it was pretty likely that a lot of people were going to think very little of me at the end of the process.

Knowing I needed a wise ear to work with me, I went to see my boss. 'I'm worried I won't sleep at night,' I said to him. 'I'm committed to making this happen, and I know that if I don't do the work to get my head around all of the noise, I'll impact my ability to really do this well.'

'Choose your coach,' he said. 'Anyone you want.'

This was a big deal and I was grateful for it. You see, if and when we were offered a coach, they were often chosen for us, or at the very least, taken from a pool of pre-approved individuals. With the freedom to choose anyone, I knew exactly who I wanted. The woman who had been modelling Queen to me for the last year. A brilliant leader and coach named Elaine Jaynes.

We met on Skype, grateful for technology's ability to connect Scotland with the USA. I remember a message arriving before our first call. One word: 'Eager!' – this was Elaine all over.

'Help me feel OK with this,' I pleaded. 'People are going to be hurt, and I'll be the one leading it.'

She smiled in that way she often did before landing a bombshell. 'I wonder why you're shooting for the Low Dream, Danielle?'

'The Low Dream?' I replied.

'Yes. The Low Dream is where the outcome is you doing the least damage possible. What about The High Dream, where you create something truly spectacular? What would that look like?'

It was a huge moment. In less than ten minutes I had a new vision: one where everyone who stayed was excited and inspired by what we would be making together, and where everyone who left felt celebrated for their achievements and supported, ready and eager to take on whatever was coming next in their life.

Before we finished, she asked me another simple question to help me sleep at night. 'Are you willing to give this 100 per cent?'

My answer was simple and unequivocal. 'Yes.'

'Then you have nothing more to give. Whatever happens, you can sleep at night knowing that you have given this all that you have and that you have set a dream that shoots for the very highest ideal you can imagine. Now, let's get started.'

It was so obvious once I had seen it. And yet, without that conversation, there would have been no High Dream, I'm sure of it. There's something about the human psyche that has us 'Play Not to Lose', and that gets in the way of our believing that things are possible when we can't see exactly how to create them.

Did I create everything I longed for? No. Of course, there were places where things didn't go the way I'd imagined: this was a complex change affecting many people. But it was a landmark in my thinking, my career and my leadership. I'm also positive it marked a major change in how we approached activities like this in the future, and in the outcome for those thousands of people who were leaving.

Shoot for the High Dream. And lean into a Wise One to help you unlock it.

Chapter 13: Sourcing Compassion

Not only do we need to get clear on the 'stuff' we're bringing to any conversation and do everything within our gift to remove it, when we're bringing our Queen to the situation, we also need to source an authentic state of compassion for the person with whom we are about to speak. There are a few key areas to unpick with this one. To be clear, whilst I'm using a professional example here once more, this applies in every conversation where what needs to be said has edge to it. At Remarkable Women we know of so many women who have transformed family relationships by sitting with these concepts and trying them in their personal lives too. The Queen is consistent *everywhere* in her life, because this is about integrity and being real. We recognise her core character in whatever setting we meet her.

The 'I Don't Want to Hurt Them' Conundrum

I've said this already, and I want to go there again. Our desire not to hurt others is almost, but not always, led by the word 'I'. Written another way, it would simply say, 'I don't want to participate in this experience'. It regularly comes with a side helping of, 'If I dig in really deep, I know in my heart that I am a core part of the problem'. Something that most of us rarely admit to. The conversation we have been avoiding for a long time is now in front of us, and we see, for probably the umpteenth time in our life, that the best route would have been to have had it much earlier. Often, what we are seeing is that if we do hurt the other human in this equation, had we been willing to respond to what we saw earlier, the hurt may never have been there or could have been considerably less. *We know that we have created this.*

In leadership, there are absolutely those conversations where we reach a sad point (again, usually having been realised long before the actual conversation), where a good, kind person is operating above their capability and we need to make a change. In some instances, we see that the repercussions of that have a high possibility of being damaging – there is nowhere else for the person to go in the organisation that would really be a great match, or they have life circumstances that mean the likelihood of someone else employing them outside of our own business is low. Maybe this spells immediate money problems, or they would have to leave the country and return to their homeland if their role comes to an end. In these instances, the conversation about to occur does not feel like Profound Service to that person at all (although it is likely to be in deep service to those who work alongside them and are struggling with the impact of their performance).

These are big things to sit with, hold compassionately *and* ruthlessly, and move forward impactfully.

On these occasions, I want to remind you of 'The High Dream' once again. The scenarios rolling through our minds focus on the Domesday outcome. We sit heavily with the questions: *What is the worst that can befall this person and will I spend the rest of my life regretting what I have done?* Our mind rehearses over and over again the disasters that may occur as a result.

If we are willing to invest our energy in what a Powerful Exit might look like for that human-being, we have the *opportunity* (if not the certainty) of creating a very different outcome indeed. In personal relationships, we can think about that as a Powerful Ending. We can always apply the High Dream.

This route takes time, attention and intention. It is not the same as holding onto a placatory belief that 'things work out the way they should' and 'the odds are good that they'll find their feet again in no time', or whatever the phrase is that we trot out in circumstances like these. In that instance, we're simply trying to soften the alarm bells in our head with words that we hope will bear fruit.

The Queen knows to navigate this important event with care, love and a true sense of possibility. This is not a conversation to be sandwiched in between other 'busy and important' activities. This is one that needs space. (A thing most of us rarely truly give, because we don't want to be on the receiving end of what might unfold: *'Frankly, it's best to have another appointment planned straight afterwards, because then I have a good valid reason to get away from this pain I have just created.'*)

The Queen enters the conversation with clarity and openness. She's ready to listen to what unfolds and having spent time imagining what the High Dream might look like for this individual. What do you know about them? What are their underlying hopes, dreams and fears? What can you do to explore those?

To be clear, the reason this takes time is that the very first conversation is often not the time to put these things on the table. I often get asked what the actual words are that I would use to say what needs to be said. It might go something like this, *'I know this is shocking and it's going to take some time to process. I expect you to feel angry about what is unfolding and I want to make it clear, I'm here, listening. I want to also be clear, I recognise that your mind is likely to start surfacing fears and concerns about what this means for you. I'm invested in helping you to work through this and in exploring what it would take for this to be a moment in your life that is significant because of what came next.'*

Take Care with Your Words

There are moments in conversations such as these, when our desire to 'fix' the person in front of us, or to remove the pain we are seeing unfold, can easily result in us either closing down so as not to see it or our part in it. We do this in personal relationships too, especially when they are coming to an end. Sometimes, our 'out loud' voice gets ahead of our reasoned thinking. We say things that can turn out to be impossible for us to honour like, 'Whatever it takes, I'm here for you,' or, 'I'm not going to let that happen to you,' and in no time at all, we find ourselves in a position where important boundaries that would have helped us to create a powerful solution are knocked down.

If you know this is your tendency, one of the muscles you are going to need to build as a Queen is about pacing, tone and turn of phrase. This is a skill for all Queens to continually develop throughout their lives, and for those of us who speak quickly and who repeatedly create the same interpersonal problems, it's one to focus your attention on early. The questions you ask, the words, pace and body language you use to respond matter. Often the Warrior could say almost exactly the same words as the Queen and create an entirely different outcome, because of the energy, speed and tone with which they are uttered. The Queen takes the feeling of War out of her words. Whenever possible, she replaces it with Love.

As a Queen, we are seeking an impactful and profound outcome in these important interactions, which means the things we say matter – not least because they cannot be unsaid. In these sensitive situations, people have long memories, especially if their Warrior is on red alert. They will actively filter through their recollections of the conversation in order to find ways to defend or retaliate.

Give yourself space to breathe in these conversations. Silent pauses are powerful (and almost always lead to the other person speaking more). Have the phrase, 'Let me sit with that for a minute before I respond,' in your back pocket (or perhaps on a notebook in front of you) so that you have a method to resist the urge to interject with some form of 'pain relief' that you will regret at a later time. We want to avoid creating a co-dependency that you become resentful of or anger at your failure to deliver on an impossible promise that you could never have met.

Take care with what you say and bring your clarity and compassion to the conversation. Serve powerfully.

Investing Time

I remember getting into a great email conversation with a man who had come to a masterclass on Queen Leadership as part of International Women's Week. He wrote to let me know that whilst it hadn't been at all what he expected (which I was delighted to hear), he was curious about what I was saying. He had many questions. They were smart and considered, and I enjoyed them so much I was willing to dive deeper even amongst a busy day – he was inadvertently helping me to think differently and to make small adjustments to the model or how I explained it. At some point in our exchange, he wrote to tell me he had decided to practise Ruthless Compassion. I'm paraphrasing because I didn't keep the email, but I remember it made me laugh: *'Everything changed because I was willing to listen,'* he wrote. *'I thought this guy was an idiot and now I see he has real things going on. Now there's a new path forward that wouldn't have been there before. This stuff really works!'* Then came the bit that made me smile, *'The only thing is, it takes time, doesn't it? I'm not sure where I'm going to find the space to keep doing all of this.'*

Ah, there's the rub.

Yes. It takes time – time that undoubtedly does not exist in your calendar. But it can, easily – if you trade it for some of those *Things that Make No Difference at All*. Because these conversations DO make a difference. Their impact is significant. Not just on the person you are speaking to, but on all those who interact with them, who are having to compensate for an issue that has not been addressed or is being ignored. The ripple of resolving these fundamental problems in team dynamics is huge. This is time that the Queen knows to prioritise.

Of course, if you've been leaving things to fester for a while, or you're leading or living in a culture which allows things to be ignored, then this is going to take longer. It's almost certainly true that for each 'people dynamic' you tend to, another will arise. But... Slowly and surely, the attention and time invested compounds until it's suddenly crystal clear that this was always the only real option to make lasting progress and impact. Now you're making the decision to create long-standing change.

As with all things Queen-like, it's a Long Game. In case you haven't noticed yet, it's also an enormously powerful one. As those around you start to see a change, moods lift, relationships improve, trust builds, and the whole system starts to shift. Ruthless Compassion is key in any relationship structure where truths are not being spoken, family and friend dynamics too. So yes, it's going to take time. Addressing interpersonal dynamics is probably the best time you'll ever spend – both in your personal *and* professional life.

Create the time first. Then see what must be let go as a consequence. Unless you are at the very top of your game when it comes to discernment, it's absolutely guaranteed that there are many things you do every single day that make no difference at all. Our inboxes and to do lists are littered with things that matter very little and that no one will even notice whether they are completed or not. One by one, drop them in favour of the things that truly matter. The beauty of this one? It's a double win because you're making changes in two places. Firstly, you're ramping up the things that count, and secondly, you're removing those that don't. It's impossible not to see significant change as a consequence.

'The Right Thing for the Business' – a Sidenote for Senior Leaders

I happen to believe that declaring that something is the 'right thing for business' is usually a code for 'Hang fire, we're about to do something very crappy to human beings and we need to justify it'. At least, throughout my 25 years of corporate life, that's what it always seemed to mean. I hid behind that phrase many times myself. It was a sign I was feeling helpless and had surrendered to something I didn't really agree with at all.

Let me also be clear, appreciating that it may make me a few enemies in the process, including those who have been dear colleagues in the past, I also believe that constant restructuring is sloppy leadership. Our aim must be to build businesses that don't need redesigning every year, or at the very least, those that don't need redesigning at the cost of human experience.

'It's the right thing for the business' is one of those phrases that we have got so used to hiding behind and using as a 'catch-all', that we've started to believe our own bullshit in the process. It's a phrase that allows us to create astounding equations and speak broad assumptions that make perfect sense until we dig into the detail. We sigh and surrender to the 'fact' that there's only one way to make things OK again, we must let people go.

The question at the heart of Queen challenges us to look at these situations differently. When we truly recognise and believe that situations we dislike are at least partly of our own creation, we have a new, much more uncomfortable lens through which to see. Let me be clear, I'm making no assumption that in the real situations you find yourself in, you have been the one deciding that resource cuts are the way to go. What I am saying is, that it's time to *own your part* in participating in a culture and operating system that has almost certainly (global pandemics aside) made your current position now inevitable.

Escaping culpability by rinsing your hands and claiming, 'It's the right thing for the business', is not how the Queen responds, if indeed she has found herself standing at this particular crossroads. In fact, let me state this to make it crystal clear: 'It's the right thing for the business' is a phrase the Queen is clear she *will never use*. She knows better.

Are there times when it is indeed the 'right thing' to make cutbacks? Honestly, I'm not so sure. Clearly, there are times when an organisation does not have the client base, the demand or the cashflow to proceed with its current level of overhead, but the truth is, I'm more interested in 1) how we got there in the first place and 2) what are the myriad of options before us in this world of infinite possibilities that would have us think and create differently?

The Queen considers both of these questions with the utmost attention, because as a Queen, her ultimate responsibility is in the care and curation of her people, in building a 'Queendom' that flourishes and thrives, and whose people are able to live a remarkable life. Throwing some of them out in order to cut costs is hardly a solution to any problem that puts people at the centre.

Chapter 14: Humans Not Objects

Another mantra to add to the Queen's growing portfolio is the brilliant, 'Humans, not Objects'. To get really deep into this one, I highly recommend reading the excellent book, *The Anatomy of Peace* by the Arbinger Institute as mentioned earlier. This chapter explains what you need to know to adopt this mantra.

The easiest way to give ourselves permission to do crappy things to other human beings in any part of life is to dehumanise them. It's easy to think that's an extreme mindset and that most of us never do it. In reality, we are *all* capable of doing it far more frequently than we might think. That's why the mantra is so important.

When we 'group' humans into large volumes that assume homogeneity (sameness), we start to lose sight of the real individuals within the mix. When we can talk about them as a 'group' with many in it, a group that is separate from us and as if all members of the group have identical attributes, behaviours and ideals, it's easy to start to treat them more as lines on a spreadsheet, or numbers that affect results, and to totally miss the fact that we are talking about actions that affect real human lives. (To illustrate the point, I came across an article recently that spoke to organisations living in the fantastical idea that everyone can have shared values. The author suggested that given the number of values available for a human to have – he stated around 500 – the likelihood of finding someone else with the same five values as you would be 1 in 255 billion people.) It's this belief that people can be grouped together and labelled with the same responses or thinking that is at the core of much of our polarization in the world. It's simply not true to believe that all Brexit voters think the same way or that those who have chosen not to take a vaccine all follow the same ideology. Grouping people together is convenient on the one hand, but for the purposes of Remarkable Leadership, a shaky bridge on which to stand.

This way of thinking shows up in all kinds of places (and to be clear, we're often not creating the terminology that groups people together so that we can mistreat them, it's simply that the terminology allows us to see them as a 'mass' that can easily have single rules or treatments applied to it). For example, you may talk about 'customers' and be referring to a group of a 1,000,000,000 or even 1,000,000 people when you refer to them. In turn, this allows you to talk about an action that might affect only 3% of customers negatively, and this allows you to believe that is a good result all round, forgetting that even in the instance of 1,000 you are talking about 30 human beings and that when that expands to 1,000,000 you are actively agreeing to 'damage' the experience of 30,000 people, all of whom have different circumstances and needs.

When we remember that we are not talking about 'objects', but actual people, living their day-to-day lives, loving their families, worrying about a roof over their heads, we start to consider our choices differently.

We can apply this thinking anywhere. Political ideologies, religious beliefs, ideas about parenting or education. Allowing ourselves to lose sight of real human beings allows us to make decisions and pass judgements that we never would otherwise. In *Braving the Wilderness*, Brené Brown puts it brilliantly: 'People are hard to hate close up. Move in.'

In order to be *truly* at peace with our decisions, it's important that the Queen keeps 'Humans not Objects' at the heart of her decision making. Whilst we might still make difficult choices, even using this mantra, we do it looking into the heart of our impact, rather than allowing spreadsheets and numbers to allow us to distance ourselves from it. It's the distance that enables us to make choices that are often far from aligned with our values.

Allowing Ourselves to Feel

In the western world at least, we have developed many behavioural norms that encourage us to distance ourselves from our feelings. To 'suck things up', or even 'man up' (a phrase with so many dangerous associations for both men and women, it needs consigning to the rubbish pile rapidly!). In many organisations, it's not 'professional' to deeply care about others (of course, we care to a point, and it's generally agreed to be important that we do, but equally, we must remember the commerciality of what we are trying to achieve here!), it may even be seen as 'soft'.

The Queen thinks differently. Whilst she is wholly aware that she cannot create a perfect world, she understands that in order to create the most powerful and impactful solution possible in all aspects of her life, she must truly stare into the decisions she is presented with. She must allow herself to feel rather than seek ways to numb out or pretend that things don't hurt. And this is big stuff. Where is the line between feeling all the feels and stepping forward? (if indeed there is such a thing).

Perhaps it can be as simple as this for now: *knowing that the ends do not justify the means*, believing that if we create solutions using approaches that 'other' someone or some group, we have not found a solution at all, we have simply created a different problem. Perhaps it can be as simple as remembering that we do not want to live in a world with increased toxicity, sadness and pain in it, and that therefore *we must take personal responsibility* for not increasing toxicity, sadness and pain through our own actions (even if it helps the bottom line). These are big, ethical and philosophical questions, yet they can be distilled to three simple words. DO NO HARM.

In order to do no harm, the Queen recognises that she must sit with the consequences of her decisions in all of their reality. If she can do that before she makes her final choice, if she can sit a little longer with, 'what else can be done?', she may just find a better alternative. And after that, another, and then another, and another.

Results and compassion do not have to be in conflict with each other. In fact, we may well find that we create more than we can even imagine from being brave enough to sit in the discomfort for longer. Certainly, that has always been the case for me – personally and professionally. First, we must be brave enough to try. That involves being willing to sit in the messy, uncomfortable and painful feelings that emerge when we look into the eye of a decision that we know is likely to induce harm in some form or other.

Black and White Thinking

The Queen knows the trap of black and white thinking. She knows that the human mind is wired to reduce our options down to a few so that we can limit the pain of decision making. She knows that it is a trap to believe that 'if not this, then it must be that' and resists the urge to pick 'the only alternative' to the very worst option, even though it is almost as bad as the first.

Working with Wise Counsel, the Queen is wholly aware that when exploring challenging topics that directly affect the wellbeing of others, it's imperative to explore multiple options. She does not have all the answers. If she is not a creative thinker herself, part of her Counsel needs to include the kind of individuals who can always see alternatives. These 'idea generators' may not have exactly the idea we need to proceed, but they get their juice from exploring different angles. They instinctively know that every problem has a thousand solutions, and they are critical for those moments when all seems lost and we believe we must make a decision that will hurt those around us, simply moving to that classic ethics problem of 'do least damage'.

When the Queen finds herself unable to truly reconcile with a decision, aligning her Heart and her Head, she knows there is more work to do. She must sit with the questions for longer. When we take action with a move that does not sit well with us, we typically mess it up – we don't want to experience it for longer than is necessary, we want it over. That has us make shoddy moves, cut corners, and generally create an air of escape. Ruthless Compassion has no place for such ego-centred behaviours.

Instead, the Queen simply sits with the question, 'and what else could we do?', holding it gently but firmly, recognising that she must slow down to speed up, in order to truly be in Profound Service.

Honouring Our Part

In his excellent book on the very topic of revisiting our approaches, *Think Again*, author Adam Grant suggests that our world has become dominated by three energies: The Prosecutor, The Preacher and The Politician.

The Prosecutor spends her time picking fault with the argument of the other. Our work becomes to prove them wrong.

The Politician is seeking to please everyone in her language by adjusting the argument to suit who is in front of her. She's playing a convincing game.

The Preacher spends her time delivering heartfelt lectures to advocate for her beliefs. She is bombarding you with passion.

These energies are not useful in a world of Remarkable Leadership and yet, of course, I can name many times in my life where I have leaned on all three (although I must confess to being especially partial to the Politician throughout most of my career). The challenge with each is they are all a form of distorted viewpoint that disowns our part in any situation we find ourselves in. When we sit beside someone for a conversation of Ruthless Compassion, it's important that we own our own part in the situation, at the very least to ourselves. Diverting attention onto why the other person is clearly 'wrong', convincing them that our solution is the best way or indeed, applying smoke and mirrors to make a message more palatable, are three routes to long-term problems. It's a critical first step to create awareness of these stances and our habit of wrapping them around ourselves before a conversation where we want to change a dynamic or the opinion of another. Whilst you may not always know how to change in the moment, a willingness to admit, 'ah, that was a politician's response' to ourselves when we are speaking, allows us to regroup, rephrase and go again.

When we focus on our need to be right, or to make the other wrong, we are on a troublesome path, and one that rarely reflects the complexities of the situation that is in front of us, or the bias of our own mind, which is constantly defending our 'rightness'. (The challenge we always have when we take that position, is that the person we are talking to also believes they are right, and so both parties find themselves in a conversation that no one is really listening to.)

The Queen listens. She knows she cannot truly be impartial. Simply knowing that, allows her to access more wisdom in each circumstance that arises.

I could give you a lightbulb moment on this one, and we're blessed with many live examples in the world where we can see the approach of convincing live in action right now. Our social media threads are full of 'Keyboard Warriors' who like to try to persuade others of their wrongness. I've done it myself and sometimes I still want to. Yet, to my knowledge, 'How can you be so stupid? Here let me show you why you are wrong!' has never changed a single opinion yet.

Why? Because most of us believe we are intelligent human beings who make rational decisions and whilst this is simply not true for *any* of us (I know! And it's still not), when someone presents us with 'evidence' that suggests we have been a fool, we are psychologically required to dig deeper to prove to ourselves that we are indeed not an idiot. This is Cognitive Dissonance at play again. I literally cannot shift to your way of thinking because in order to do that I would be demonstrating to myself that I am not smart at all. What I do instead is look for more evidence to suggest why I am right.

Instead, when we tune into 'where am I stuck in a single position that I cannot be moved from?' we can be honest about our own unreasonableness. Our own ability to listen. Instead of trying to get the other person to listen to why we are right, we can own that we might be missing some information too. The Queen is willing to ask herself the question, 'If I was wrong about any part of this, what part might it be?'. You might be surprised at what you uncover and how much more powerful your conversations are as a consequence.

Chapter 15: Empty Apologies, Promises We Can't Keep, and 'Flannelling'

Even when we think we've cleared out all our own internal noise so that we can truly show up for the other, there are three obvious places where we can start to see leakage. Empty apologies, promises we can't keep, and 'flannelling'.

These three approaches show up differently and yet they are all showing that we are avoiding experiencing the pain of the others who are with us in order to protect our own feelings. In these three scenarios, we've made it all about us again.

Empty apologies are rife in our lives. You may struggle to notice when you're doing it (so often the case for us humans), and I know for sure you'll recognise it in others. Empty apologies say sorry whilst immediately shifting the blame back to the other party. In essence, they're saying something like, 'I'm sorry I did this, but you made me do it because of your behaviour'. Oddly enough, these kinds of apologies do exactly nothing to resolve the situation. Usually, they inflame it more.

I experience empty apologies coming from me as something like that old game Minesweeper. You may remember it if you're as old as me. I used to play it in the days where I was a secretary with not enough to do and a need to make myself look busy. It was a tiny little screen game (great for removing swiftly and pretending you're doing real work in the event of a manager approaching) that was a bit like a more sophisticated version of battleships. In essence, there were a number of 'mines' hidden behind blank squares and your job was to clear the full screen of mines without blowing any up. When I find an empty apology coming out of my mouth, it's literally as though I have inadvertently stepped on a mine. I can often be half-way through the sentence before the other half of my mind is saying, '*No! You didn't say that in your out-loud voice, did you?*'

I know what's coming next. Trouble. Pain for both of us. Of course, as I'm doing it, the feeling flowing through me is real. It appears to be an inherent part of human nature to do everything within our gift to not experience 'wrongness' internally, and so there I am, in full Prosecutor mode, looking for the things the other person has done wrong, to justify why I have also misbehaved. In an empty apology, there is no apology at all.

 ## Lightbulb Moment: A Big Apology

We were in the midst of that huge restructure again. A week or so earlier, thousands of people had been brought together in smaller groups to watch a video of me and my boss sharing what was about to unfold. In the middle of the video, I had done everything within my gift to honour the experience of those who were watching. I had said something along the lines of: 'I want you to know I recognise how challenging this is going to be for many of you. I care about what happens next and I'll do everything I can to make this as smooth as possible for all of you.'

I did care and I wanted to make it clear that my door was open, that I wasn't going to dodge the hard stuff. Some managers had watched the reel several times as they brought in different members of their team to watch.

One afternoon, one of my Heads of Department came to see me and then another. They wanted to make me aware that one particular manager had said on more than one occasion something akin to: 'If I see Danielle say she cares one more time, I'm going to go and punch her in the face.' They wanted to let me know that they had it 'under control'.

Whilst I appreciated the intention from the team and their loyalty to me, I asked them to back off, to let her experience her anger.

Hours later, I received a message from her – a brave move in itself, given the hierarchy. She asked to meet for coffee and I agreed.

Her assumption was that I was angry with her based on what I'd heard. There was some defiance in the conversation and also a genuine approach from Queen. She wanted to speak her truth and, hard though it was for me, I wanted to meet her where she was. In my head, I was speaking to myself over and over again, 'Listen without defending, Danielle, listen without defending.'

'I am so disappointed in you,' she said, moments after making it clear she was not there to apologise for what she said. 'I had so much faith in you, of all of our leaders. How could you get this so wrong?'

It was a punch in the gut. I don't know what I had expected, but it wasn't this. I don't even know where the words came from to be honest, I was so in the moment, experiencing her anger, disappointment, fear and frustration.

I breathed deeply and leaned forward. 'I'm so sorry,' I replied. 'I knew when we started this programme that it was impossible to get it right for everyone. I'm beyond sorry that I got it wrong for you.'

She looked back at me, exhaling immediately. What came next was unexpected too.

'I think that's all I needed to hear,' she said. And with that, the conversation was over. I sat at our table in the canteen a little longer, processing what had occurred, sad to my bones that she had been so deeply impacted by my choices and actions, hardly able to comprehend the power of an apology without excuses.

In that moment, even if I had managed to refrain from an apology that pushed the problem back to her (inviting her to consider whether her behaviour had been appropriate as a senior manager for example), it would have been easy to make promises I couldn't keep to alleviate the situation. To 'Politician' my way out of the scenario with a bunch of things that I was unlikely to be able to enact, but could make sound good in the moment. For sure, my natural tendency to want the best for others can lead me there too. I want you to feel better. Immediately.

Making promises we can't keep is *all about us*. It's another way we try to avoid the pain of the other person, especially when we have played some part in creating that pain ourselves. For the most part, people can sense it too. They also know full well when they have been 'flannelled' by a leader who does not want to speak the truth aloud.

Flannelling (where we use bland but fluent talk to dodge an issue) is as prolific as empty promises. It occurs frequently when we rely on process to get us out of a problem that really requires an honest conversation – we allow people to apply for promotion for the tenth time, knowing that they have never had the true feedback that means the job is simply not on the table. We encourage people to take out formal grievances that almost always damage the career of the person raising them, when we know deep down that we have chosen to opt out of dealing with the deeper issue. We tell them they just need to develop a little more and then they will be seen differently. We know it is not true, but it sounds as though it might be to both of us.

For a Queen Leader who wants to be in Profound Service, empty apologies, promises we can't keep and flannelling are behaviours we stay conscious to avoid. They leave deep imprints on the memories of those we engage with. They erode trust in ways that are difficult, if not impossible to recover from.

Watch Out for the Things You Make Up

The human mind is an absolutely incredible machine. Nothing we have ever invented comes even close to this wondrous organ that can perform unimaginable computations, actions and filtering of information. The Queen is wholly aware of the fact that even the most brilliant brain comes with limitations. Like so many things in life, the design elements that have the most genius in them, often cause unintended problems too.

In many ways, the human brain is a tool of reduction. It absorbs millions of 'bytes' of information and filters them in an instant to allow us to make decisions whilst avoiding having to think about all of the key elements of a decision each and every time we have to make it. It essentially stores data that allows us to 'shortcut' our thinking, drawing on past experiences, habits and its own mechanics to present us with a 'simple' solution or next step.

That's beyond useful for so many things. Imagine how much energy we would use if we had to physically and mentally apply ourselves to simple routine activities like brushing our teeth or drying ourselves when we get out of the shower. We don't have to apply much, if any thinking, to these actions in order to complete them. In fact, I bet if I asked you to tell me the order in which you dry yourself with a towel, you'd struggle. But when you get out of the shower, unless you're suffering with an injury or problem, I also guarantee that you dry yourself in exactly the same way every time. The mind is quite astonishing in its ability to generate instructions and actions without us even noticing.

Where it gets problematic is that it can also join dots inaccurately and present us with *faits accompli*, which are, quite simply, nothing more than assumptions. This is happening pretty much *all of the time*. Our ability to distinguish between 'fact' and 'opinion' is quite limited on occasions. We regularly believe that we absolutely understand how others think and that we are 100% accurate in knowing their motivations.

Operating from this assumption is dangerous, and an idea we need to avail ourselves of immediately. The Queen is wholly aware that it's challenging enough trying to understand *our own* motivations without moving to the giant leap of faith that is assuming we know why others do what they do.

When we make up stories about other people, we play out actions as though they are true. I have a brilliant example in my life of someone distancing herself significantly in our relationship because she fervently believed that I had discarded our friendship, based on a story *she had entirely made up* about what I was thinking. Nothing could have been further from the truth, and when she finally plucked up the courage to, quite angrily, declare me as a bad friend, I genuinely looked at her with surprised eyes – I literally had no idea what she was talking about. I'm also beyond grateful that she was brave enough to have the conversation, given that she passed away less than a year later. Our friendship was restored easily and swiftly to its former glory, but wow, was it a lesson in understanding how often we live with made-up stories that we believe to be true.

We make stuff up about other people *all of the time.* And it's exactly that, *made up.* Honestly, I can't tell you how many times clients try to persuade me that they know exactly how someone else is thinking and what they will do next. I also can't tell you how fun it is to ask them to check out their assumptions and see what they report back with. Sure, sometimes they're right. But in truth? They're also utterly wrong. Far more frequently than you think.

All of this means the Queen knows that in a world of Ruthless Compassion and Profound Service, she needs to find out whether the stories she has made up are true or not. She needs to be highly aware of the difference between actual facts – *Her name is Danielle* – and evaluations – *She won't take that job if you offer it to her, it's not what she wants, I know it.*

How do we find out what's true and what's not? Well, that's pretty easy…

But I Haven't Made Anything Up!

One of the things I love most about Ruthless Compassion is that in many, many circumstances, it is SO much easier to apply than the 'difficult' conversation that has us spinning round in circles. In fact, I'm pretty sure I decided to develop my skills in this place because I simply couldn't bear the thought of another one of those conversations that made me feel sick to my stomach at the thought of it. You know the ones I mean, I know you do. They have you awake in the middle of the night, playing options over and over in your mind. They distract you on almost every turn. At least they did for me. Truth? They still do on occasion, but I can promise you, it's so rare these days that it almost surprises me when it happens (and when I go back to 'how am I creating this?', well that's always a facepalm moment as I realise the inevitability of my own choices).

Often when we talk with our Queens in Training and share how to check out their long list of assumptions, I get the impression that they don't believe me when we describe it as easy. Of course, every muscle takes time to grow, but even so, I promise you that this approach is ridiculously effective. Like many Queen actions, I also recognise that the way to do this is incomplete without practising our *tone and phraseology*. The energy we put behind words is often more important than the words themselves. It's hard for me to demonstrate that in a book, but I hope you can understand what I'm alluding to. Good Queens are learning from other Queens all of the time. There are women in the world modelling this on a daily basis. Look out for them. Notice how they are showing up. Better yet, come join us on a masterclass at Remarkable Women – we offer several a year that are free to participate in – and watch us modelling as best we can what that looks and sounds like. The more we can cultivate our ability to speak and write questions and answers in an open, honest and loving fashion, the easier this becomes.

When it comes to the stories we imagine, our first move is to sit down with the question, *'What am I making up about this person or this circumstance?'* In the beginning we'll do this before, or after speaking with the person in question as we grow our muscles in this space. Over time, the question will come naturally. Heads up on this one though. It's super easy to respond to this question with, 'nothing', and that is so very unlikely to be true. (I want to say its 100% unlikely to be true, but that wouldn't be true either of course – at least I can't know it to be. I can share that literally hundreds of conversations with women and men from all walks of life tells me it's very, very likely indeed that you are making *something* up.)

To be clear, there's no need whatsoever to beat yourself up for the fact that you make stories up and then live like they are true: that's a human experience and like I said, a powerful tool of the mind. What we want to shift to now as we strengthen our Ruthless Compassion muscles (and any place where we are in relationship with others) is an awareness that we do it, so that we can be alert to it and make smart modifications accordingly.

If you truly can't see whether you are making anything up at all (or indeed believe you're not), start with the things that are irritating you or you're worried about, or where you're absolutely sure you're right. That might look like this:

- *'There's no point having this conversation, I guarantee you she won't listen to a word. She's fixed on her position.'*
- *'If I sit down and have this chat, she's going to burst into tears and manipulate the conversation, that's what she always does.'*
- *'There's no point asking if I can do it. She's made her opinion on the subject totally clear. I'm wasting my time.'*
- *'I just can't give her this feedback. It will break her.'*

Once we have all of these concerns and supposed certainties on the table, the great Byron Katie offers us a lens through which to explore them. It's my favourite model for checking the things I'm making up vs the absolute truth or fact of the matter. (She famously calls it 'The Work', and it's for many more things than this exercise in Ruthless Compassion. She offers The Work for free at www.thework.com should you want to explore further. For now, let's just stay with this small element.)

There are four questions in The Work:

'Is it true?' (Answer yes, or no. No need to say more.)
If your answer is no, then we already know we're working with an assumption, something you're making up. No need to go any further. Thing is, you're pretty likely to argue it is true. Which is why we move to Question 2.

'Can I absolutely know that it's true?' Note the 'absolutely' here. I like to think of this as, 'can I be 100% sure?'

In my experience in applying Question 2, I see it's pretty rare I can be absolutely sure. And that gives me a clue I'm living with some assumptions.

'How do you react, what happens, when you believe the thought?'
And here we see all the juiciness of assumptions and what they bring to our own actions. We've made a thing up (even if it's a perfectly logical and rational place to find ourselves, it is still made up to some degree, based on our connecting of dots and what we think we know), and now we're running around acting as though it's true.

What that often means in the case of Ruthless Compassion is that we start to plan for expected next moves from the other person, and in the conversation itself, we can easily find ourselves looking for validation that our assumptions are correct. This also means it's pretty easy for us to miss vital clues as to what is really going on.

When we think we know the answer, we simply go looking to check that we are right. When we are offering true Ruthless Compassion, we are far more interested in understanding what is really at the root of the problem, than validating our own smartness and clever calculations.

If you can't get your head around what I'm saying here, Question 4 may help:

'Who would you be without the thought?' In other words, 'If you didn't believe this to be true, what would be different then?'

Perhaps you would be more curious, or less agitated or nervous about the conversation. Perhaps your anger or self-righteousness would disappear. Perhaps you would simply become open to understanding more. Since we have already established you have made a story up, now you get to see the impact of the story on you and potentially your relationship with the other person.

So, now what?

Ask Rather than Accuse

I've been using the technique I'm about to share with you for so long and have found it so easy, that I'm always a little bewildered at the fear that sparks in many people's eyes when I suggest that the route to checking out assumptions is to ask. Even when I share the way to do it, I experience a deep-rooted fear in so many that this cannot be as effective or pain-free as the way I portray it. I've learned over time that there is no place for persuading (the Queen is compelling and inspiring, but never convincing!), I simply show up, model and teach. You get to choose what to do from there. Of course, like every single technique in this book, I'm asking you to grow a muscle. At the beginning you can't imagine having full strength there, and if you show up and keep practising, it won't be long before you see a significant difference. In fact, I have a lot of stories to tell with this one. For now, let's get stuck into the simple technique of asking (with a neat little twist, of course).

I do know that part of why many people look at me like I'm a person from another planet when we venture into the 'asking' territory, is because they have a fear of the 'ask' being thrown back in their face. And in some ways, I think that's justified. Often, we think we are *asking*, when what we are really doing is *accusing*. And when we accuse, what happens? The Warrior comes out in full force.

'Did you do this?' will regularly get a defensive response. 'I believe you're doing this, are you?' will usually fare no better. Most of the time, we use some version of the above. Sometimes, we layer onto it an accusatory tone of voice, or, in trying to be 'nice', we show up as passive aggressive.

Humans can smell accusations a mile off. It brings out our defences.

The turnaround is simple. In order to avoid an accusation, we have to own that we have totally made up this part of the story. That our question comes from something we have jumped to in our own conclusions, and that in fact, we have no idea whatsoever whether it is correct or not. The onus of 'blame' is on us, not the other person.

The phrase we use to ask the question owns that we are making things up and brings it back to us. It might go something like this: *'I'm making up a story that you've had enough of working here and would rather be somewhere else, but I realise I have no idea whether that's true or not. Would you share with me your perspective?'*

Or: *'I realise I constantly make up in my head that you'd rather be in another department, but I've never really checked it out with you. Have I got that right or am I miles off the mark?'*

In these scenarios, the 'gun' of accusation is off the table, I'm simply curious and recognising that I probably don't understand you at all. Sure, sometimes it turns out my assumptions are in the right ballpark, and even then, I want to go deeper, test the next level. There's always more to learn about the person sitting in front of us. Once we share that information together, new options reveal themselves that simply may not have been there before. Of course, this means that not only do we need to get clear of our own stuff, drop our need to be right and check out our assumptions, but we also need to *lose any idea that we already know what the outcome looks like.*

Chapter 16: Co-creating the Outcome

'Convincing' is not that far away from 'accusing' when it comes to human reaction. I was shocked years ago in my corporate life, when I was invited to attend a course on 'Convincing Communications'. It was literally a facepalm moment for me. Every senior leader in the organisation had been invited to attend, based, I assume, on a continued conversation that we were all appalling at having 'difficult' conversations (which was absolutely true).

And here we were, in a room learning how to convince people. Why would we want to *convince* anyone? The Queen is not a convincer. Rather she is compelling, inspiring, aware, agile, receptive. Yes, she has a vision, but she does not give her attention to how she can persuade others that she is 'right'. Indeed, she is utterly open to the fact that there could be an even better way out there. She believes in setting a North Star for her mission – a broad brushstroke, a bold ambition, but she knows that others will have contributions that bring something new and improved to the conversation and the action. The last thing she needs to do is convince. Those who come with her come because they feel it in their bones too, this is something they want and believe in. She compels. Others choose accordingly.

 Lightbulb Moment: Throw Away the Notes

Back to that training room. Clearly, I wasn't exactly there as a willing participant, although matters were helped by the fact that I knew the trainer well – he had trained me to appear on the Consumer Affairs Complaints Show a year or so earlier, and had also been part of a team who helped us to build our messages as we moved into another big restructuring of the organisation. I liked him a lot (and he was astonishingly skilled at getting me from 'rabbit in the headlights' in front of a ruthless journalist out to get his soundbite, to someone who was wholly aware of how to navigate the game of 'Catch me if you can' that I endured for over four hours of filming days later), and I did not like the journalistic methods much at all. You see the nature of his own background in journalism seemed to mean that he operated as a 'Politician' to use Adam Grant's earlier model (page 115). What he was really teaching us was how to 'win' by presenting a picture that was truthful in words, if a little shadier behind the scenes. And here he was, teaching us to convince. You can understand why I might have been a little skeptical.

We were each handed one of those awful role-play sheets. If you have ever managed people, you're a lucky person indeed if you've never had to go through the horrors of a manufactured conversation in the form of role play. My sheet laid out the context of a scenario with one of my team, and made it crystal clear what I was to say and the only outcome that would be acceptable. We definitely were not doing Ruthless Compassion. More passive aggressive JUST DO IT. Muttering to myself, I picked up my pen to take notes. As the most senior person in the room, I had decided it was unacceptable to derail the class with my thoughts on why this was the worst idea ever, and that I would simply try to do the best I could with what was presented to us. (Looking back on this one, I'm pretty sure my Victim had at least some control over the steering wheel and that's another story.)

Moments later, I found myself sitting in front of my 'team member' (who I had in fact managed several years earlier and who turned out to be an astonishingly good actor). I picked up my notes and began to work through them (all the while being filmed so that it could be played back to the rest of the group). Moments in, I looked him in the eye, said, 'I'm putting these down, they aren't helping one little bit' and dropped my paper to the floor.

Leaning in, I asked, 'Tell me, what's really going on for you? I'm making up that this is a pretty stressful situation you find yourself in?'

For the next five minutes, we explored. He did a great job of not capitulating and we probed together and began to have fun. At no point did I resort to the solution offered on the piece of paper. I did not say the thing that the brief clearly said must be said. We closed the conversation and joined the rest of the group where we carefully dissected every conversation.

A month or so later, I discovered something astonishing had happened. Several of my team had been on the course after me and one day, I was offering my not so positive feedback about it in a less than Queenly way. One of my team laughed, 'That's funny,' she said. 'You obviously don't know that the whole course is centred around your video now. It's the model we've all been invited to follow.'

I've got to be honest, I toyed with whether to share this story with you, given it feels like one of those humble brags, that isn't so humble at all. Yet I know that stories often bed in points better than explanations, and this was a telling moment for me. I had actually returned to the group expecting to be called out for doing it 'wrong'. It felt like a significant moment when I realised the penny had dropped for at least the guy at the front of the room, and perhaps some of my colleagues too.

When we don't know all the facts, we can't possibly know the outcome. Having a fixed end-state, closes the myriad of possibilities that are available to us. It assumes there is only one way and we can work it out for ourselves, even though we must be lacking information about the context of the other person or group. When others perceive we are guiding them to a specific destination, and that we are simply listening in order to discover what we need to drive our point further home, they either resist or surrender. What they rarely, if ever, do is reconcile.

Hold On. This Takes Time.

Co-creating a solution is challenging when we're not used to it (to be honest, even when we are it has its moments!) – some of us are used to getting our own way, or thinking we know best, while others amongst us are used to capitulating or 'compromising'. It takes intention and presence for a Queen Leader to really listen, explore and open up to possibility – and often, more importantly, to slow down the conversation so that she can really own when a solution has been presented that is clearly a 'fudge' or an attempt for both parties to close the discomfort of the conversation down fast.

The Queen is more interested in a way forward that is truly meaningful than she is in getting out of the room – even when she knows it feels uncomfortable. In a co-creation scenario, where Ruthless Compassion is at play, she has a powerful role to play in noticing the energy in the room, the body language and the subtle facial expressions that suggest, 'I'm agreeing to this, but I'm not really bought in.'

Ruthless Compassion comes into its own when we slow things down and are honest with what's truly occurring. I would posit that we almost always know that we haven't truly reached a satisfactory conclusion, it's just that mostly, we want to ignore it in favour of exhaling again and getting out of an awkward situation.

There's a great term in the legal world called Willful Blindness. A CEO, or other leader with legal responsibilities can literally be found guilty of actively choosing to look the other way to avoid being implicated in something that they suspected was happening (to truly explore more on this concept and how it plays through in our behaviour, I highly recommend Margaret Heffernan's excellent exploration on the subject, aptly named, *Willful Blindness*).

Throughout all of her Service, the Queen is acutely aware of Willful Blindness in her own actions and behaviours. She acknowledges her own human tendency to look the other way when something feels sticky (or she is tired, stressed, frustrated, and any other number of agitations that have us want to pretend something isn't happening).

When it comes to 'How am I creating this?' in relationships, Willful Blindness is an easy place to spot our own part in the problem. In this particular scenario, the next step is simple. Call it out with compassion. 'We could move on, but I think we'd be kidding ourselves. I sense you're agreeing with me, but it also seems it's not a reflection of how you really feel. What am I missing?'

At Remarkable Women, we have a real life 'Bullshit Button'. It literally says 'Bullshit' in about 10 different (and amusing) ways. Of course, it's not always the moment for such a button, and most people who've been in our world for a long time, know it announces itself with a hugely loving intent.

 ## Lightbulb Moment: A Moment to Moment Choice

Several years ago, Nic and I were facilitating a day with a group of senior leaders looking for another step change in their thinking. Although we don't do much tailored work like this anymore, we had agreed on the basis that we had prior relationships with some of the people involved. We spent a powerful morning together, before stepping into the topic they had asked for specifically. They wanted to explore the real action they needed to take in order to facilitate the next level of change they were longing for. Or at least, that's what they said they wanted.

Frankly, we should have known better than to follow their urgency. But we did. The outcome was predictable.

The large group broke into three smaller groups, and whilst we had given them an unusual and interesting way of creating their action plan, it was clear within 30 minutes that the energy had been sucked from the room. Sure, they were doing what we had asked, and dutifully putting their actions up on flipcharts, but it didn't take a genius to realise this was not going to plan. A day that had begun beautifully was about to fizzle out. It seemed pretty clear that everyone was up for pretending that it wasn't happening. Honestly, we were considering it ourselves.

Nic looked at me, 'We need to call bullshit. But then what?'

'I have no idea,' I replied. 'Literally no clue. But we know better than to let this continue.'

The groups returned and the first began to share their actions. Moments in, I leaned forward and pressed the small red button sitting in front of us. 'Bullshit detector, bullshit detector,' our merry button announced to the room.

For a moment, everything stopped and all eyes were on us.

'Our guess is that you have zero to no intention of doing any of this,' we offered to the room. 'Is that true?'

It was pretty awkward. But it didn't take long to perceive a giant collective exhale. We had no idea where to go next. Yet, for a further 90 minutes we created something new, together, slowly shifting to another level of truth. Uncovering what was underneath the 'froth' of a desire to generate action. By the end of the session the energy was palpable again. Did we have all of the answers? Of course not. But we had well and truly moved on from pretending that we had agreed a collective way forward.

The Queen trusts her intuition. She stays with what's occurring, knowing that problem avoidance always creates a bigger problem in the long term. She keeps a watchful eye on her own tendency to Willful Blindness.

When There's Something that Has to Be Said

Perhaps you're thinking there's a missing piece of the puzzle here. The bit where you say the thing you know you need to say. The actual hard bit. It's all well and good doing all that listening and discovering what might be going on, and of course, there's also the part where you speak your truth and/or make it clear that there are some boundaries about to be laid out. In my experience, this often feels like the sticky part. For some of us we skirt around the edges, listening carefully and responding to what's being said, whilst knowing there is a missing piece of the puzzle that renders the solution incomplete, or sometimes, completely out of sync. For others, we blurt it out fast, desperate to get this piece out in the air and the rest of the conversation runs amok consequently. How do we get clear on what needs to be said in order to lay the foundations for a powerful conversation?

It may seem odd that I've put this question at the very back end of the section on Ruthless Compassion, because it comes sooner in the process, right? Or does it…?

In reality, it's important to have explored the other aspects before we get to establishing what 'must' be said. Without sourcing compassion for the other person and getting clear of all our own noise, it would be easy to bring our Warrior to this section. Without being clear that we cannot possibly have all of the answers to the very best outcome, it would be easy to present a *fait accompli,* 'This is how it's going to go, whatever you say next', and so we find ourselves creating the same problems we have come across so many times.

Having processed and cleared our own noise and opened our heart to new possibilities, we can now sit with what really needs to be said. Again, there's so much power in tone and phrase. 'I want to be clear, it's time to find a different way and what's happening currently is off the table as a way forward' can be said just as easily from a Warrior voice that creates defensiveness as with a Queen. We can all spot a saccharine sweetness that is inauthentic without even trying. We've all been on the receiving end of passive aggressive statements. Don't be that person.

How you say what you say matters, just as much as the words you use. Sourcing compassion for the person in front of you, stepping into Profound Service for them is the way in which we offer words that others can hear.

The human instinct is so very smart. We all know when someone does not want the best for us, or is afraid, or saying what they've been told to. And we all exhale a little when it becomes clear to us that the person sitting in front of us deeply cares about what happens next. Somehow, it enables us to hear even the toughest message. It's almost as though someone has finally called out the elephant in the room. We might not wholly love what we're hearing but, for most of us, there's a sense of relief too. We no longer have to keep up the charade or the bravado of pretending that everything is OK.

Whilst I'm going to give you some examples here of turns of phrase that may work well, of course it's impossible for me to cover every given scenario and to touch on the one that you feel you need (I can almost feel the hope rising that you'll strike it lucky), so I also encourage you to actively look for Good Queens and Kings in your life that you can learn from. Who are the people around you who show an innate ability to say things that no one else can in a way that has others sit up and listen? If you can't find them, look out into the wider world. Capture the brilliant phrases when you hear them, start to make a habit of learning from those who are doing it already. Yes, it takes time, and as you already know, this is a Long Game. I'll say it again, it takes time to become a Queen. There's always more to unlock. The good news is, every time you take a step in that direction, you're going to realise you're on a path that's worth following. Things are going to get easier. You're going to become more impactful. Your life is going to change for the better. Once you commit to this way of Being, there's no going back – who would want to?

The Words We Use

Like I said, this bit takes practice. Marshall Rosenberg, the creator of *Non-Violent Communication*, argued in his early work that our language is full of violence towards each other. The first time I saw him (on video as he is no longer alive), I felt this was a bit strong and yet over time, I see it constantly. Phrases that have made their way into common parlance can actually be a little shocking if you think about their core meaning. I will always remember the moment I read a sentence in a book asking why on earth we would want to 'kill two birds with one stone' and yet, to this very day, still finding it entering my consciousness as an appropriate description to verbalise. We often talk about 'hating' people or things whilst we energetically pass the blame for our own feelings onto someone else who is simply getting on with their life. In heated discussions we say things that we can never take back.

It's simply not true that 'sticks and stones will break my bones, but words can never hurt me'. Most of us can easily recall a time in early childhood where a comment or judgement was given to us that left a scar that may even be there to this day. Of course, we can absolutely learn not to take things personally, but at some point, we all have an experience of doing exactly that and my guess is, that if you're a human walking this planet, you have used words as a weapon many times too.

Rosenberg also claimed that we spend a lot of our lives making 'demands'. His definition of a demand is critical. He describes it as a request of someone when it is clear to both parties that the person requesting will only accept a yes. As I've said before, words matter and so does the energy with which we convey them. In fact, Rosenberg suggests that we can only expect two responses from a demand – Rebellion or Submission. Read that again. It's a gem. The only responses we can expect from a demand are either *Rebellion* or *Submission*. Now you know it, you're going to see it everywhere.

The Queen does not seek submission (and of course, is not drawn to the idea of creating a rebellion). Whilst the Warrior will almost always see that as a victory, the Queen knows better. Submission leads to reluctance, sabotage, gossip, collusion, apathy and all kinds of other reactions that are not helpful or transformative in creating a solution. We may get what we desire in the short term, but we have won a battle and re-engaged a war. The impact of rebellion goes without saying.

Queens do not make demands because they understand they do not lead to lasting change. A Queen recognises that every single human being has agency and will make their own decisions in their life. What she can always do is set boundaries and explain consequences. In terms of the words we use, they may look something like this as an example:

'I understand that you have the ultimate decision about what you choose to do next. You're the boss of you after all. What I want to do right now is be clear that I am also making decisions about my own actions and boundaries. I'd love to talk about a way to change the situation we find ourselves in. And let me be honest and say that without a change in this dynamic, I will make a decision to step back from our relationship.'

I remember once having a similar conversation with a former brilliant boss of mine. I had made a request, and he had come back to negotiate.

What I saw clearly was that I was not willing to negotiate. I also knew that he was often an excellent and skilled Warrior. Moving into battle would leave me scarred, whatever the outcome.

I returned to the conversation. 'I want to be clear with you, I'm not open to negotiation here, I want to know if you can meet my request without adjusting the parameters of it. Are you willing to?'

Unsurprisingly, he responded, 'What if I don't?'

Finally at peace with my position (it had taken a good few of those Shitty First Drafts to get there), I replied, 'Then I'll need to consider what that means for me.'

'Aha!' he cried, 'So you're threatening me with leaving?' (Despite my measured language, you can see how most would find themselves responding in this way, right?)

'Actually, no,' I responded, 'I'm not threatening anything. I'm simply asking whether you can meet my request, and acknowledging that if your answer is no, then I have more thinking to do.' I meant it. There was no threat. And of course, it was entirely possible that one of my potential decisions in the event of a no, could be to resign. But my energy was different. I wasn't throwing a grenade on the table and saying, 'now choose'. I was simply asking for a truthful response so that I could assess my options and use my own agency to decide what happened next.

He must have realised at some level, that I was not making a demand, because we were able to move on in the conversation and talk more. We were able to stay with the challenge of both wanting different things. Eventually, we co-created an outcome through listening and talking together. It certainly was aligned with what I needed. I don't entirely know how he felt about it because we never had that discussion. What I can say is, in my eyes at least, our professional relationship continued to flourish. There was no underlying resentment, rebellion or submission between us. It certainly felt as though all was well.

You know if you are making a demand. Honour the other person's ability to make their own decisions. Make what you need clear and allow there to be consequences without the threat of war.

Nuanced? Oh, yes. Takes practice? Always. Will it create change? You'll be astonished.

A Way of Being

The tone of our voice is one of the critical places we convey Ruthless Compassion. I believe that *How* we say what we say matters as much as, if not more than *What* we say. If you go back to that story I've just shared, where I use the phrase, *Then I'll need to make some decisions accordingly*, I'm confident it's easy for you to play that through in your head as an aggressive, threatening or even sulky response. In fact, that may be exactly as you experienced it when you read it.

Ruthless Compassion requires *authenticity*. You cannot 'act' out your compassion, love or care for another – they will know in an instant it means nothing. It's not a 'tool' you pull out of your toolkit to manipulate a situation in your favour. Without truth and real empathy, your 'planned' conversation will head off in all kinds of directions that are messy and destructive. Even if you 'win', you may shake your head and say, 'What a nonsense this ruthless compassion is, it didn't work!'

The path of the Queen is not for those who are unwilling to bring their Heart to their leadership and their lives. Those of us committed to mastering Ruthless Compassion are learning how to navigate our emotions, our innate sense of rightness and selfishness, and our constant need to defend and protect our position. We are learning to spot when we have mis-stepped and own it, to create boundaries and stop pleasing, to step through the challenge rather than find a convenient shortcut. Our work is to get this into our bones, and make it so natural as a response that we resort to our less effective (but habitual) tactics less and less.

Remarkable Leadership takes remarkable intention, remarkable attention and remarkable commitment. It takes ownership and accountability to a new level. Ruthless Compassion sits at the very heart of the change we are all longing to experience and create.

We're ready to move to the final Foundation of Queen Leadership. Before we do, breathe, regroup. Give yourself space to reflect. Write on the pages and do your thinking here with me. Ruthless Compassion offers you avenues for change in all of your relationships in life, not just work. If you are willing to play The Long Game, this approach has the potential to transform so much.

CORE FOUNDATION THREE:

SLOW DOWN

TO SPEED UP

Chapter 17: A Million Miles an Hour

I'm laughing as I start to write this section. I can't imagine a single person who knows me well describing me as someone who should be teaching how and why to slow down. I'm the woman who types so fast that no one else can use my laptop because there are no letters on the keys. I wore them all off within a year of purchasing it. When new people come to work with Remarkable Women, it takes no time at all for the query to arrive, 'How do you get through this so quickly?' 360 feedback in my corporate life often said, 'It can be really hard to keep up with Danielle.'

The truth is, I laughed and smiled every time I got that feedback. At some level of course, I knew it wasn't helpful, and at a deeper level, I believed that it was part of my 'secret sauce' – one of the components that made me highly successful throughout my life. At some level, I still do – it trips me up all the time.

This section is for all of us, but it's particularly for you (you know who you are), the one who is just like me – hooked on her speed and ability to make things happen, reveling in the recognition and accomplishment that brings. If you can, slow down your reading for a minute, because I have something to say to you.

Your gift of speed brings with it a shadow when you push it too far. You know this. I don't know how it shows up for you but it's there, softly whispering in your ear, inviting you to stop running at everything with such urgency in favour of smarter, more effective, more impactful moves.

I'm here to say this: You. Can. Do. More. More than you can even imagine.

And what do you have to do to *really* meet your potential? To do more than is beyond your wildest dreams? *You have to do LESS.*

May I offer you a proposal? You already know the well-trodden path. The one where you race at all the things and churn them out at the speed of light. Are you willing to give me just 90 days to experiment with something new? Negotiate me down – what are you willing to try? Give me your number. Write it down here. Make it a little more than that, just for sport.

And hang on a minute, there's another woman I need to have a word with. Your friend. The one who thinks she has to do all the things for everyone. Ah, there you are. This section is for YOU too. You might not go so fast as your speed-addicted friend, but you also love to pack in all the things, right? Now I've got your attention, let's begin.

Addicted to Speed

We live in a time where speed is highly prized. The last 20 years have seen enough innovation to match the 100 or more that preceded them. Our lives resemble the science fiction films some of us grew up with as children. Flying cars are predicted to become a multi-trillion-dollar industry. We're seriously making plans to live on other planets. And of course, there's more to come. 'Faster' is an emblem of success. It's rare you would hang out in a meeting in a business and hear the words, 'How can we slow this down?'

For many of us that way of Being permeates through everything we do. We run around like crazy things trying to fit more into our days. We know we should stop and smell the roses, but somehow we can't bring ourselves to get around to it until we've got one more thing done. When we finally do stop, there's no energy for rose smelling. Instead, we pick up our mobile phones and allow our thumbs to entertain us. Scrolling for a morsel of something (who knows what exactly?) because that seems to be all we have left inside us to do. Without intention, many of us would struggle to actually watch a TV show all the way through, although we might have the screen on all night. My truth? Sometimes in our house we actively choose programmes in a foreign language so that we have to pay attention to the screen!

The Power of Distraction and Manipulation

We've got too clever for our own good. Whole companies dedicate their attention to tricking the brain and hooking it into things it would never choose. We may not be addicted to illegal substances, but we've been more than willing to hand our brain over to devices that are designed to keep us going back for more. It's hard to filter out the useful from the useless because the very design that offers both to us is designed to grab our attention and reward us with a hit of dopamine that simply makes us want more.

Notifications are everywhere we turn. Even if we switch off all the beeps and buzzes, our inbox still calls us with unread emails pointed out in bold. The tiny envelope at the bottom of our screen suggests we might be missing something very exciting indeed. Maybe you've bought a watch that vibrates to let you know when someone is communicating with you. Try as you might, you cannot outwit these systems. Many, many brains have given their very best work to ensuring that you keep coming back for more.

This isn't a section about social media, or any of the other places we are being conditioned to act and think in certain ways. There are other people who can do that so much better than me. No, this section is about raising your excitement and curiosity around what we can access when we learn to *slow down*, in spite of the fact that our minds are most likely following habitual patterns that are absolutely not serving us. Consciously hooking ourselves into systems that tell us what to think, what to spend and where to put our attention is an 'interesting' choice.

As I've said before, the Queen is deeply discerning.

In this section we have much to explore. Where I can, I will offer you resources that have helped me dig deeper in the places I know I need to pay attention. For now, watch for a mind that resists and rebels like a Warrior (*this is nonsense, it's not really a problem, I'm strong enough to do it my way and I like doing ALL the things*), and that folds and gripes like a Victim (*I can't possibly work against a system that is designed to make it hard for me, it's just not right that we've let things come to this, someone needs to fix it*), and remember, the Queen, *creates* her life.

That means owning, with love, that we are creating the situation we find ourselves in. The one where we are too busy and can't stop? We did it. The one where we 'have' to do that thing? We choose it. The one where we have to do that thing because no one else will? We believe it.
When we're willing to see that and explore what might be possible if we took a different path, infinite possibilities open to us.

And that's a lot more fun than scrolling for likes on the internet. At least, I think it is.

Instant Gratification

We're wired for instant gratification. It's not useful when it comes to how easy it is to manipulate our actions through our mobile phones and other devices. It's also less than helpful for those of us who want to create a big impact. We've talked about the Long Game before and I want to bring it back here in the Slow Down to Speed Up section. You see, one of the things I regularly see women do when they set themselves a mission is then run out of steam when it hasn't taken a giant leap forward in the next six months or year. Somehow, we take that as a signal that we can't do it after all.

The beauty of the Queen as a metaphor is that by virtue of her position in life, she finds herself in a Long Game whether she likes it or not. The Queen is a Queen until she doesn't exist anymore. There's no 'getting bored and trying something else', instead there's only the simple beauty of focused attentive action.

We all know that when we look at the stories of other people's accomplishments and lives that we are not looking at reality. Yet it's funny to me how often we are fooled by what we read and see. The world is showing us 'instant success' every day in the media and online. It's selling us ways to get there too. The instant gratification trap is an easy one to fall into, especially for those reading this book who already have a sense that they're not enough. It allows us to fall into Victim mindset: *What's the point? They're well ahead of me and clearly better at it than I am. Who am I to do this when so many people can do more than me?*

The Warrior in us might throw our plans out of the window with ruthless vigour: *There's no point to this one! It's clearly not the one. Onwards!*

Staying in our lane is critical. Falling for the supposed success of another is madness without the context to back it up. Social media makes it very easy for us to build our credibility online and often that success we deduce from what we see, is incredibly different behind the scenes. I can't tell you how many times I've had conversations with early-stage entrepreneurs who thought winning an award was going to save their cash-strapped and struggling business, only to find that it was just a moment in time and that it made very little difference at all. To bring it back to a personal level, I work with women starting up businesses regularly who have all kinds of stories about how much money our business makes and how profitable each of our product lines are. It's a shock to them to discover that we were running for four years before I paid myself a full annual salary. In comparative terms in our industry, we have generally been ahead of where we should be and for sure, we have created some brilliant products and gathered a community of incredible (remarkable) women around us, but I guarantee all is not what it might seem on the outside.

Results compound over time. Just as a rocket takes 80% of its fuel to get off the ground, big missions take time to gain momentum. But when they do, they move at pace. Commit to a longer game. Don't fall for the voice in your head that says: *This is going too slow, it's never going to work.* Remember you have time. It is worth the time. You might even start to enjoy it…

Believing we are going too slow is a trap. Wanting the buzz of success 'now' has us play small. All of us can find more shallow levels of success every single day if we choose to. The bigger stuff takes longer. It really is that simple.

Chapter 18: I Am Creative Before I Am Reactive

In all of my leadership career, people talked about Time to Think. Usually, along the lines of, 'If only I had more time, then…' combined with a giant sigh. I don't collude in that conversation any more. Hear this with love: time is not the issue. Time is the handiest excuse on the planet for not getting things done. In my experience, when I drill down into this conversation further, it's not time I find as the culprit at all.

Most of us seem to be downright terrified of a blank piece of paper. So much so, that it is enormously more reassuring to settle down with our inboxes, or to fill our diary with endless meetings than it is to do 'Quality Thinking'. What does Quality Thinking even mean?

I'm a strategist at the core of my strengths and nothing pleases me more than time in the diary to really Think, and even I can struggle in that moment between getting started and doing nothing at all.

And yet, Thinking, truly sitting with a challenge and allowing our creative juices to ponder and reflect is a core skill of the Queen. She knows that she can easily divert herself with all kinds of distractions to feel busy and accomplished and yet, without clarity around what is important and what is not, she could tick a thousand things off a list and yet have done very little at all. More challenging still, it's highly likely that our working environment and practices are set up to have us respond to the many alarm bells that are ringing urgently in our inbox and on our mobile phones each morning. You know this of course; I highly doubt I'm sharing anything new.

'Give me six hours to chop down a tree and I will spend the first four sharpening the axe,' Abraham Lincoln is quoted as saying (there's some debate over the number of hours he went with, but you get the principle). When it comes to Queen Leadership, we like to reframe that in a simple mantra we have adapted from someone clever in the world (it's not always so easy to know who started something), '*I am creative before I am reactive.*'

In practical terms, for me, that actually means that I choose how my day starts before the world decides where I should put my time. My first hour at my desk on a working morning is mine, without my inbox and without any 'tasks' to do, except to capture some of my current whirlwind of thoughts in a journal and then to identify where my attention will go for the rest of the day. On a Friday, I use some of that hour to look ahead at the whole week and to give myself just a moment to decide on priorities.

Some of you are rhythm creators and will be drawn to this idea, and some of you will be laughing already, 'not another one of those books that says get up at 6am and 'Zen' yourself for the day!' No, it's not. This is what works for me. I am by nature a person of discipline and routine. Whilst many of my clients often want to learn how to be more like that, it's easy to see when I dig into their whole life to date that actually, my way of living would drive them insane. They don't want routine and standardisation and process, even though they'd like their perception of what the outcome of that way of Being is.

In our own way, however, we can notice our desire to be impulse led (reactive) vs wisdom led (creative) and this is where the Queen comes into her own. Responding to impulses has us feel better momentarily, responding to wisdom creates peace of mind and a sense of progression.

Creative not reactive can simply mean that in a given moment, when an idea seems like a brilliant one, we simply agree to sleep on it and see if we are so excited tomorrow, or to take a short break to reflect and notice whether we have been swayed by a swelling of energy and support.

If we do not take the time to choose where our attention and intention goes, then no one will do it for us. If we do not take a moment to go within and be with a question for a little longer to check its validity, no one will do it for us. If we insist on reacting and responding to the demands of the world on a daily basis, then we will find ourselves circling round the same questions and meeting the same dead ends on an incredibly regular basis. The Queen forges her own way of honouring her commitment to putting what matters first: her own style of creativity before reactivity.

The Blank Piece of Paper

For many of us, the blank piece of paper (or indeed, screen) is terrifying when it comes to that moment where we have made space to be in reflection and creation. It's beyond tempting to respond to the siren call of the inbox, where at least it feels as though we are actually doing something when we respond to a request or see that ever-filling inbox number drop for a second or two.

We are not all strategists, and even those of us who are, have never really been taught how to think in a powerful way. There's an illusion many of us allow to rule us that says, 'Ah, if only I had the time to think properly, if only *we* had the time to think properly, if only we had the space to slow down, *then things would really change around here.'*

The Queen doesn't fall for that trap. When that message starts to rise up in her, she knows a more interesting question is of course, 'How am I creating this?' followed usefully by, 'What am I really resisting here?'

As a natural strategist, I'm aware that the real sticking point for me is the point where there is literally nothing, followed by the next point where what I have is a total mess and makes no sense at all. My desire to have all of the answers, tied up in the neatest bow that I can then present to 'The World' has me look longingly at my phone in the hope that it will save me from this torturous moment of simply not knowing.

The blank piece of paper is a tough moment. For me, the answer is to make it fun. A screen serves me less well than a giant sketch pad and felt tip pens. I'm no artist, but there's something enjoyable about colours appearing on a piece of paper, something that hooks me in and has me stay longer. I suspect that writers who still choose the clickety clack of old-fashioned typewriters or who even choose to write with a real pen have learned the same thing.

If we are 'making' ourselves use tools that simply do not inspire us, then of course we will head in other directions, drawn to the lure of an immediate fix vs that thinking time we were apparently longing for so much. Yes, you are doing important work. Yes, for some of you, you are literally attempting to change the world, and even so, the Queen knows that to do her best work she needs to give herself full permission for it to be fun.

If you need a thought partner, find a thought partner. If it takes an inspiring space and new stationery, use it. If you think best in the shower, or out on the trails, build that into your working life. If books and podcasts trigger your thinking in new ways, factor them into your creative time. For goodness sake, unless a blank piece of paper or screen truly fills you with joy and inspiration, dedicate some attention to 'how' to best think, rather than kidding yourself it's simply a case of creating the time.

You can do this. You will have more 'strategy' and 'creativity' in you than you think, and most of us, need to accept that there's a requirement to learn *how,* rather than be frustrated that we don't have some innate immediate talent. Like most things Queen, this is another Long (and worthwhile) Game!

The Power of Compounding

Acceptance of the infinite possibilities that rest in The Long Game is at the core of the Slow Down to Speed Up principle. I'm no mathematician (this is an understatement in the extreme), but the Queen understands inherently that results compound over time. The analogy of the rocket using 80% of its fuel to get off the ground leans into the same principle, as does the idea that an acorn takes many years to turn into an oak tree. These analogies, metaphors, constructs and clichés are plentiful in our lives for a reason. They connect to a larger truth.

BIG THINGS TAKE TIME.

After the immediate rush of a big idea, the bit that follows, the earlier part of the mission establishing itself if you like, can feel like wading through treacle. Things just don't move fast enough for many of us. Thinking that speed is of the essence may regularly lead us to give up, believing it's not worth the effort. However, if we lean into the idea of compounding, we can take huge heart from a mathematical truth that we do not need to 10X or supersize anything (contrary to popular opinion). If we put our attention on doubling our impact each year, it doesn't take long at all before we see things are transforming at a rapid and almost impossible rate. Compounding our impact requires several attitudes from the Queen.

The first step is developing our ability to Stay. Wow, is this a biggie for most of us. I really want to honour that. It's hard to stay with something when it doesn't look like it is flourishing. The voice in our head can drive us wild with messages that we are a failure and that we should indeed move onto something else.

The highly unconventional and successful entrepreneur, Derek Sivers, writes in his book *Anything You Want* that he will never invest in an idea. He wants to see a commitment to execution. He offers a formula (check me out with the maths again) that combines brilliant ideas with the quality of execution of the idea. It's obvious really that a good idea that no one knows how to execute or can be bothered to start is literally worth nothing, but I think I had never really explored that an average idea well executed could in fact do quite well. Of course, the ideal is a brilliant idea, brilliantly executed, but even an average approach can surprise us with its ability to thrive if we stick with it for long enough.

The good news about this is that we don't have to sweat about having the best idea in the world, (because many of us can spend a long time doing nothing while we wait for that one), we simply need to get started and stay for long enough to see what might emerge. Our investment in the idea for a longer period of time, gives us permission to learn, adjust, think again. Owning that there's no chance our mission is perfectly articulated in the first round or indeed that we absolutely know how to make it happen, combined with the truth that an average idea can get traction, allows us to move forward with grace.

You know what your soul is calling for you to create. Lean in. Stay the course. Give your acorns time to root and grow.

The Wisdom of Possibility

We often say that the only thing standing in your way is your mind when we're teaching our Remarkable Women. If not the only thing, it's almost certainly the biggest thing (even though you might protest otherwise).

Why do we say that? Firstly, as I've said before, because the mind, brilliant though it is, is a reductionist tool inclined to black and white thinking. There's so much data and information out there that we would be overwhelmed if we tried to take in every stimulus and byte that was presented to us in each and every moment. In order to counter that, the mind develops systems to group things together, to look for repeat patterns and to enable us to do many things unconsciously (ever had that moment when you arrive at a place wondering how on earth you drove the car to get there since you can barely remember it? That's your mind doing what it does).

That ability to segment and reduce things down to the familiar is an incredibly useful tool. We need those filters to get on with our lives and to be effective. It also comes with a massive disadvantage. We can lose sight of the many possibilities that are out there. In fact, the country we have been born in, the family we grew up in, the messages we have been 'conditioned' to by the media we choose to access or indeed the advertising we are all subject to, are all adding to that problem. We see the world through a familiar lens. And that lens limits our thinking. It has us believe there are certain ways things should be done. In order to fit in and belong, in order to be 'successful'. Even though at some level, we are aware that many things are possible, for most of us, our mind will revert to the same patterns of thinking when we are presented with problems. Often that thinking is pretty black and white. The reductionist element of the mind is fond of 'it's this, or that' without thinking about the literally billions of options that are available in any given moment. That might sound like a huge exaggeration, and yet if you know anything about variables and combining them, you can see this to be true very quickly. It's just that the mind rules out options as 'silly', 'impractical', 'dangerous' or 'too hard' by reverting to its memory bank of what it already knows. Quite literally, we will do things largely, 'the way we have always done them' – even those of us who are extremely creative.

How do we change this? Well, that's pretty hard on one level. Because we know what we know and that's where the mind returns to. Where the Queen starts is by recognising that just because she cannot work out how to do things, that does not mean there is not a way to do it.

Since the dawn of time, (wo)man has been doing impossible things. At least they seemed impossible when they started. It would have been beyond ridiculous to our grandmother's grandmother to imagine a world where we swiped right on screens to access information on practically everything that exists today. Back in the day, we did not know how to fly, we just believed we could.

That belief is at the core of unlocking potential. The Queen believes in possibility. She understands the limitations of her mind (and of those around her) and when something seems impossible, she is wise enough to understand that it's pretty likely that she simply cannot access an easy answer. She is simply willing to stay in the enquiry. To get curious. She is excited about opening new possibilities.

This simple mindset reframe is beyond important when it comes to Remarkable Leadership in the world. Once we realise how limited we are by the patterns and routines of our own environment, by the way the systems around us are setting unwritten rules, we open up possibilities that we could never access otherwise.

Lightbulb Moment: Surprising New Ways

A brilliant friend of mine runs a hugely inspiring and impactful venture that finances and supports women entrepreneurs who are making a difference on the UN's top goals. They are renowned for doing things differently. However, even she was astonished and delighted with the response she received when she recently made an offer to an indigenous Canadian woman to join the leadership team.

The woman had asked to replace the contract she was offered with her own. In her contract, she explained that she would work according to the seasons of the year. That what she would do in Spring, would be different to what she did in winter.

My friend, shocked at first, realised that this was yet another place where she had fallen for believing that there was a specific 'way' to do things. She started to get curious about what it would mean to run their annual cycle of business differently. She began to see that even her creative mind was missing all kinds of opportunities to create new ways of working that had always been right in front of her.

The mind is brilliant at taking you to the swiftest answer it understands. And once we know that, and can see the limitations that occur accordingly, we can seek ways to open up our thinking. To imagine entirely new solutions.

The Queen knows that there are more routes than she can imagine to what she wants to create. This means that when she finds herself with only two options in front of her (and one of those is terrifying and the other is pretty awful), she knows she has only just begun the exploration.

Urgency vs Wisdom

Slowing down to speed up requires a Queen to notice that there is a significant difference between urgency and wisdom. In this world where everything needs to be done 'today' and we can order things to arrive in our home just hours later, it's easy to believe that it's important to address the things our mind says are urgent.

Understanding that urgent does not mean important or wise is a game changer in how we show up in our daily lives. Urgency is often a signal that comes from the Warrior in us. Wisdom emanates from the Queen, who recognises that very little is urgent at all.

So, how do we distinguish between the two? A good chunk of it is down to that voice in our head and the feelings that run through our body. When we believe something is urgent, we might start to speak faster, move faster, discount suggestions in a hurried fashion and get frustrated when an answer doesn't appear quickly. We may feel a sensation of butterflies running through our body or a tightness in our shoulders. Our body literally begins to react to the perceived 'threat' of an 'emergency'. Our patience decreases and the Warrior in us starts to push things through. Warrior meetings in organisations often have a sense of 'we have to make a decision in the next hour, whatever happens!' and, somehow, we all get suckered into believing that declaration is indeed true: that without the pivotal decision, something (we know not what because we don't give ourselves time to reflect on it) is going to go horribly wrong.

The voice of wisdom often offers shockingly *unremarkable* advice. That's because in any moment where wisdom appears, the invitation from that softer, calmer, refusing-to-be-drawn-in voice inside us is to slow down. Wisdom appears in the form of a whisper that says, *Let's take a break. Half an hour to reset and refocus won't make any negative difference at all. In fact, it might just give us the breakthrough we're looking for'.*

The voice of wisdom will tell us, this is not urgent, not urgent at all. It will encourage us to breathe, find a way to calm down, settle the atmosphere in the room, perhaps even to address what is underlying the frantic thoughts and behaviours that are emerging in us or others around us.

Very little is so urgent that it can't wait. Yet our bodies and minds can be inaccurately primed to tell us otherwise. For most of us, our best ideas will not come under extreme pressure. They will come when we allow space for our subconscious to process freely. They come when we allow ourselves to 'sleep on it'. The Queen knows what a remarkable difference a night to process can make.

At Remarkable Women there's an unwritten, regularly invoked rule. If we find ourselves debating a position for too long with no agreed outcome, we simply say, 'Let's give it 24 hours and see how we feel tomorrow.' Inevitably, by the next day, we have managed to filter out the distracting noise of urgency to find a simple, clear and obvious solution. It's usually also clear that had we listened to the voice of urgency the day before, we risked creating a solution that didn't match our needs. We risked unsettling others and disrupting plans that didn't need to be disrupted, simply to settle a false alarm going off inside us. Wisdom will almost always have you slow down. Back to that tree chopping analogy – be careful you're not trying to cut down those trees with cutlery knives.

Many of us are guilty of doing busy work foolishly. The Queen knows better than to respond to a demand of urgency. Even when her body and mind are desperate to persuade her otherwise.

Chapter 19: Asking for Help

I wrote about this one in *Remarkably Easy*. Except let me be clear, I have to write about it and think about it so many times, that I don't for one minute think that asking for help is easy. At least, it's not for me. You see, Warriors love to go it alone (because no one can do it better than them) and Victims don't believe anyone will help them anyway (often because they've asked really poorly several times before and this has become a self-fulfilling prophecy). I like to swing between the two in the moments I most need help, believing that *it's quicker to do it myself* and that *I mustn't intrude on people's lives and they'll probably say no anyway*. There's so much to unpack here.

If you truly want to have a big impact in the world, it is madness to think that you can do it alone. It goes back to that 1+1 formula (page 42). As a collective we can do so much more than we can as individuals. On a rational level, we know that. It's as clear as day that none of us are so talented that we can do all the things. In addition, many of us are more creative as a consequence of being with others, and our thinking is often hugely and helpfully provoked by being around those who are smarter than us in their own fields. Most of us understand that when we're in a good space, because then we're not really 'asking for help', we're creating together.

Often that principle falls apart when we've backed ourselves into a corner. When something feels hard or we don't know a way out of a problem, it can be a natural tendency for at least some of us to withdraw and feel we have to fix it ourselves.

Equally, many of us may have had an experience of asking for help and not getting what we need.

That's why, as part of any teaching on Queen we offer in the world, we also teach what it means to make a Powerful Request. It's one of the key tools that every Queen is continually learning to cultivate and master.

The Powerful Request

Learning to ask for things in a way that enrolls and inspires people to come with you, sponsor or endorse you is critical for any Queen. We all need help and support as we step into bolder impact in our lives. Once we learn the skills of the Powerful Request, we cannot help but get better at it, because there are a few core components that easily change how we show up.

The simple first shift is moving away from Lazy Requests. (Get ready for this one, because it's pretty much guaranteed that you make some of these all the time.) How do you spot a Lazy Request? Well, let's take the ones I reckon you will have received at some point in your life. In this world of easy access to messaging details, it's likely you've been on the receiving end of plenty of them.

Sometimes, they're scattergun in their approach (fling as many out there as you can and hope some stick – a bit like 'cold calling') and sometimes they are well intended but poorly executed. You recognise them most easily by the effect they have on you.

Lazy requests are the kind of request that makes you sigh inside, or that irritates you deeply. You know, the ones where someone asks you for something, and it feels like they haven't seen you, understood you, taken you into consideration, or bothered to explain what they need and why. If you're the kind of person who says yes out of obligation, you may still say yes to some of them (depending on who they are from and your degree of loyalty to them), but they don't make you feel good. In fact, even on saying yes, you're likely to feel the resentment rising.

If you're anything like me, you might even feel frustrated at feeling as though, in the spirit of treating people as human beings who make mistakes, you now have to take the time to say 'no' when it feels like whoever has asked you hasn't really put in any effort in the first place.

These requests come in all shapes and forms. They particularly come by email (because that seems to be the easiest way to ask for things badly), and they often look like they've been 'cut and pasted'.

They're the ones that make you feel as though you're one on a list of many. Often, they ask you do more work than the sender has done themselves (you know, the ones where a template has been created for you to fill in that makes the sender's life easier, but yours a lot harder?). They are regularly vague in their request, 'can you run your eye over this?' or 'can I pick your brains about that?' These kinds of requests are everywhere. And whilst they drive most of us totally mad, we don't seem to have noticed that we create them too – because somehow, we have learned a way of asking that is ineffectual, even lazy.

When we write one sentence on a social media post asking for people to sponsor us and then wonder why they don't, that good old question, *How am I creating this?* comes to the fore. When we send someone a random 'follow this page that you know nothing about' request, we have lost sight of WHY it would be useful for the person we are asking. When we crash out an email in 30 seconds that isn't thought through at all, why are we surprised, even indignant when we don't get a response? We ask for 'favours' and wonder why they don't land. Then we tell ourselves some made-up story like people don't want to help, forgetting that, as always, we are at the centre of the challenge we find ourselves faced with. As always in Queen Leadership, we need to look inward.

Queens know that at the heart of enrolling others to help them is the idea that they need to make a Powerful Request – a request that has even those who say no, feel delighted to have been asked and supportive about what it is you're trying to create. A Powerful Request takes skill and intention. As a topic it could be a book in its own right, but we can easily get started here with some simple principles:

What are you asking for, why do you need it and what you are going to do once you get it?

Banging out an email (to make yourself feel better about asking, or to get it off your list) is going to have exactly the impact you would imagine on the person receiving it. So, before you go hurtling off asking for help, set aside some time to CRAFT your request – to give it the intention and attention it deserves. All too often, we try to enrol people into something we know we are not vested in ourselves and have no intention of completing.

Be specific about what you are asking for

Regularly, we ask for *vague* things 'I'd love your thoughts on whether the narrative catches your attention and speaks to people like this…' is a far more useful request than, 'Could you take a look at my website and tell me what you think?' plus, it ensures that my attention goes to where you really need it and you don't get equally as vague an email back from me that says, 'It's great – well done you' (which almost certainly means, 'I haven't really looked at it, but I want you to feel as though I have.').

When we ask to *'pick someone's brains'*, it can make a huge difference to explain specifically what we're grappling with and what we'd like to bounce around. That way, I can be clear when I receive it as to whether I have the time or energy to dedicate to the request and indeed, whether I'm the best person for the job.

When we ask for an *introduction* to someone, we want to consider whether we are indeed ready to spend time with them and to consider whether that introduction would be beneficial for the other person too. I'm not suggesting a 'trade' here, what I am saying is the other person should be as excited to meet us as we are to meet them, otherwise, why would they meet with you? To be sold to? Who wants that? Queens are smarter than that. They consider whether this truly is the moment and why the introduction could bring a smile to everyone. They make the request from that place.

Ask without expectation

My former coach, Rich Litvin, co-author of *The Prosperous Coach*, has this great line, 'Needy is creepy, Danielle,' he used to say. 'Don't be that person.' It's so much easier to make a powerful request of someone when you have no expectation that they will give you a yes. The Queen knows that whilst she absolutely needs others to support her in creating whatever she is choosing, success never falls on the shoulder of one very specific person. If they say no, someone else will say yes. What that allows her to do is ask in a way that doesn't lay guilt or obligation or expectation onto the other person. That matters. Even if you think a certain person is really the ONLY person who can help you, layering guilt or manipulation into a request (no matter how subtle) means that of course, you might get a yes, and that it is highly likely that yes will come with a degree of resentment. And when someone doesn't really want to help you, the help you get is not so powerful at all. Plus, next time, they'll be super wary of responding.

Don't get what I mean? Think about all the times in your life that you have said yes because you felt sorry for the person or there was guilt around saying no. Were you able to show up for them joyfully and happily in your gift of help? For most mere mortals that's practically an impossibility. When we feel cajoled or persuaded into something, it's hard to give freely. Queens know that kind of help is far from useful.

However – and this is important – there's a significant difference between asking without expectation and saying someone's no for them. Requests that start with, 'I know you're busy so if you don't have time for this then I totally understand' are simply operating from an assumption that you have already got a no. They are not powerful by any stretch of the imagination. Once again this is about crafting your request. Often, I will use something like, 'I want to be clear; I have no expectation that you will say yes to this. I'd love to have you with me and I want you to want it too. You'll know if this is something you really want to support and I totally trust that.' See the difference?

Make it personal

Cut and paste mail merges don't cut it in the world of the Powerful Request. They miss out on context or on the different ways that individuals with different skills and resources can help you. Human beings want to be SEEN. Using your request to have someone feel understood and chosen means that whether they say yes or no, they feel great about having been on your list, rather than one name on a list of many. Mass requests tend to have poor impact because they have been de-personalised. I'm not asking anyone in particular, I'm hoping someone might step in. When we ask no one particular, guess who responds? Exactly.

Understanding someone's context and how much time or resource they have to offer can make a real difference to your request. A great place to start is asking yourself, 'How could this person help me in a way that would have low impact on their time and resources, and high impact on what I'm trying to create?' is a great place to start. At the very least, making sure you do some of the heavy lifting (rather than creating a request that looks like an offload of work) is going to make a difference in how it is received and whether someone really offers the help they can. A cut and paste or hurried email asking ten people for feedback on your new website, misses the nuances of each individual. One may have an eye for aesthetics, one may know your ideal clients, one may have a great eye for mistakes and detail. Bringing forth that talent in your request allows them to be seen and to recognise the value of the help they are offering.

And yes, of course, personalised requests take longer. That's the point. If you can't be bothered to spend time on it, chances are, you're not that invested in what you're asking for anyway. Feeling like it's a pain in the butt is always worth sitting with a little longer.

The Powerful Request takes practice. It requires a degree of honesty with ourselves about our motivations and intentions, and our commitment to what we are trying to create. If this all feels too much effort already, then that's good news, don't start. If you really want to create magic, sitting with the question, 'What would make this a powerful ask?' is guaranteed to take you further forward than you ever would using your current methods.

Slow down to speed up. Put your energy where it makes most difference. Show up as a Queen. Ask in a way that enrolls. This is worth your time, for the multiplier effect it can create.

Chapter 20: Protecting the Asset

Take a pause before you embark on this section. Why? Because it would be easy for you to let it pass by: to say, 'I know this already, I've seen it a thousand times before.' If that's the choice you make, you're going to miss something critical in the Queen's toolkit.

What is it? This Asset that needs protecting at all times?

You. You're the asset. Not the thing you're trying to create, the work that you're doing, the team you're leading, the family you're supporting. *You.* If the asset breaks down, falls over, runs out of juice, implodes, then everything else stops. If the Queen insists on doing everyone else's stuff before her own, then the Queen's work never gets done. The impact she is committed to creating becomes half-baked and is fuelled with whatever energy she has remaining. If the Queen insists on treating this Long Game like a series of 100m sprints, then her 'personal best' is going to get slower and more ineffective with every day that goes by. Yes, you'll get things done (the Warrior in you will make sure of it), but there will be a cost. In fact, more likely, many costs.

An exhausted Queen who insists on 'pushing through' creates consequences all over the place. Her decisions are less sound, she makes mistakes, she upsets people, she does half a job, she leaves chaos in her wake.

I've noticed over the years that it's beyond hard to appeal to women to look after their health. For most, it's almost impossible. Heck, I've been the woman lying in bed, fresh from spinal surgery, unable to even sit up, let alone walk, with a laptop propped on my knees, insisting that I just 'have to get this done'.

So, I'm not going to appeal to you to look after yourself for your sake, because I know you'll just push through anyway. I do want you to see that you *do not do your best work when you have not paid attention to your body.* For some of you that means nourishment, movement, energising yourself. For others, it means less cardio, less discipline that must be followed at all costs, less competing with yourself, less pushing through.

People around you pay a heavy cost when you have decided to keep pushing through. When you rush a decision using a tired mind, you make calls that can have repercussions for weeks, maybe months or years. You can have people doing things on a whim that frankly, never needed to be done at all. When we speak from frustration and tiredness, our ripple effect can be more significant than we can even imagine. A sharp, ill-considered word here and another there can do damage that we might never see but is nevertheless still there. We are not our best selves when we are pushing through, ignoring the signs of our body to make different choices.

It's not about you. It's about everyone else. Imagine the difference in organisations if all of their leaders were fresh, focused, clear, energised. Really. Stop and think about it for a moment. The change would be huge. 'Busy' would be replaced with 'Wise'. Ruthlessness could finally be married to compassion. The possibilities are *endless*. Exciting. Without doubt they would change the world.

It starts with you, protecting your asset, so that YOU can be the best leader you are capable of being. It's up to you to make sure that as far as is humanly possible, your ripple effect is a positive one, so that you can truly say, 'I gave this my best shot'. And to be clear: your 'best shot' is not remotely the same thing as running your fuel tank to empty.

We want our good Queens to live for a long time, and we want their lives to be blessed with clarity, focus, purpose and love. This means that protecting the asset is a non-negotiable – not to be messed with under any circumstances. It's not a bubble bath and gratitude journal thing that can feel trivial when positioned incorrectly. It's part of how we change the world. Who knew?

 ## Lightbulb Moment: Pushing Through

At Remarkable Women, we found ourselves recently in a tricky situation. Emerging from one stage of the global pandemic we all are familiar with; we had a number of brilliant clients who had been waiting a long time to attend one of our retreats. There were four sets waiting to attend who had already been delayed twice. In addition to that, many of our clients had waited well over a year to be with us in person for a live event.

In the moment, we made a decision to put all of the retreats together in a three-month window (we would normally run three retreats over the course of a whole year) and to sandwich the live event somewhere in the middle. At the same time, we were releasing a forthcoming Remarkable Leadership programme in line with our usual schedule.

It was a lot for a small team, especially when you include within that context that two of the four retreats would be running against a new format we had never used before, and one of those was also in a new venue. (New venues take up much more energy because there is so much unknown about how things will flow, what will work and what will not. Even with the best planning, something always crops up.) On top of that, we knew from past experience that retreats take a lot from us. We find ourselves gratifyingly exhausted at the end of them. Gratified yes, but exhausted all the same.

Still, in lieu of almost two years with no live interaction, we were eager to get going. We figured we had enough tools in our bag to ensure that we could offer a brilliant service to our clients and not keel over in the process.

One retreat in, with another looming, we discovered that was a very wrong assumption indeed. The new content took more effort from all of us to deliver (including our support team), because we simply didn't know it yet. Launching a new programme in the midst of that with all of its usual challenges was becoming overwhelming, and our inboxes were filled with enquiries for the live event as well. By the end of the second retreat (which was spectacular), I was grouchy, argumentative and so tired I felt like a phone whose battery had run to zero. I had no idea how I could rejuvenate and deliver the three more events that were coming. I wasn't the only one feeling that way.

What was clear was that we were all planning to turn our Warriors on for the next 8 weeks and then recover once we got to the other side. We were reverting to that time-honoured tactic of 'suck it up as best you can', and that was clearly a terrible idea. We needed to bring our Queens to the fore. This was a classic example of allowing the ends to justify the means and even in our tiredness, we knew better than that.

We sat down and played the 'Can/If' game. 'We CAN be rejuvenated at the end of this process IF…' and we offered our ideas into the room. In the end, the way forward was simple and clear. 'We can if we invest more money in the problem,' Nic said eventually.

I sighed with relief, as did the rest of the team. It was obvious really, but somehow it had taken us a while to get there.

Whilst it would have been nice to make good profit from the retreats, in reality, they were not significant in our revenue plan for the year and, in fact, we had had a better year financially than we could have imagined. We could easily put some money aside to bolster the team and bring in more hands that had more energy than us.

So, that's what we did. Two months later we concluded all of our events with great pride. Not only had we not fallen over with exhaustion, but generally speaking, we had the same levels of robust health that we would normally have. Our clients had had an exceptional experience, and we had not traded our skin or blood in the process. We had protected The Asset.

I've said it a lot in this book, and I've been teaching and coaching it for too many years now to be daft enough to think it has landed, so let me say it one more time. *There's ALWAYS another way.* ALWAYS. You are not the exception to that. That thing you think you absolutely have to do, exactly the way it has been laid out – it's a lie: a lie you're telling yourself. If you're struggling to get creative, the next section may well hold the clue. There's always another way. Just because you can't see it does not mean it's not there.

Swimming Against 'The Vortex'

In a world hooked on 'busy', it seems so much easier to do what everyone else is doing. 'How can I possibly step out and slow down when everyone else is charging around like a mad thing?' you may be asking.

I get it. Truly. When we're stuck in a 'Vortex' of everyone doing the same thing, swimming against it looks like an impossible task.

You can take my route of learning if you like. Wait until your body takes you down (although I know now that it's pretty easy to override even that powerful message if you're determined to) before you realise there was another way all along, or you can simply choose to *create your life* – one tiny step at a time.

It's a fallacy to believe you need to wake up tomorrow and change *everything.* You're in it for the Long Game.

Change something.

Tweak it in the tiniest way. Take one thing out of your diary. Choose to be in a conversation for longer. Like I've said before, run tiny experiments. Let the growth compound. See what happens. If you're willing to play, my hunch is that you're going to be astonished at what's possible.

Chapter 21: The Power of the Wisdom Council

As I bring this book to a close, it's critical to talk to the power of many to create impact again. This time in the context of the Queen's Wisdom Council, that you may have noticed I have mentioned more than once already. Many of us with high Warrior tendencies have an inherent desire to go it alone. It's a bonkers strategy. Not least because the scale of what many of us want to create in the world or even in our organisations, is far greater than one individual. But also, when we get locked in our head and insist on doing it one way, my way, we can get lost in our own nonsense. We can start to believe that we're 'right' and push on at all costs. We can lose sight of the perspective of others and the fact that our own mind is tricking us all of the time.

The Queen knows there are moments she cannot be trusted to truly 'do the right thing'. I don't mean moments where we suddenly become a 'bad' person, but simply that each of us is human. We're addicted to our own ways of doing things and some of those ways are pretty daft indeed. Some of us can't be trusted to step away from a problem and end up gritting our teeth through solutions that are pretty sub-standard compared to the ones we would have discovered had we taken a breath. Some of us can't be trusted to turn our phone off or ignore emails when we get home at the end of the day (even though nothing important is happening at all). Some of us can't be trusted not to take our people down with us in a blaze of glory. The list goes on and on.

Knowing that we cannot always trust ourselves to do the right thing, good Queens create a Wisdom Council around them: a circle of people who will not collude, and who will challenge and offer new perspectives. These are the people who see our nonsense and hold us higher, who have expertise in areas where we do not, people who are capable of slowing us down or speeding us up, and of speaking with Ruthless Compassion. The Queen does not need Boot Lickers, she needs Kings and Queens around her who will challenge her and whose advice she trusts, because it is so powerful.

She needs a Wisdom Council.

Some of us need people who inspire us, some need those who will give us a loving kick in the behind, some need those who will look us in the eye and say, 'no'. Some of us need people who call us out when we are behaving badly. Some of us need the ones who can see new ways forward. Some of us need ALL of those people and more.

From today, start to look for your Wisdom Council, and bring them to you intentionally and with permission to call you forth. Something exciting happens in the world when people bring their talents together to create something far bigger than they ever would themselves. It gets even better when those are the kind of people who want to be on a mission like yours.

When we hang around with those who agree with us that 'it really is terrible around here and they are such bad people for doing this to us', we spiral downwards. Gossip has no place in the Queen's world and nor does colluding in any story that the circumstances we find ourselves in are 100% due to the actions of other people. We might kid ourselves that those conversations make us feel better in the moment, but that satisfaction is akin to that of a cigarette or a shot of tequila. It's not going to get you where you want to go.

So go, find the others – the ones you long to spend more time with – the ones who love to chew on the same problems as you with excitement and creativity. Draw them together and invite them to be part of something bigger, or simply to be part of your support system along the way. Choose them with discernment. Like a Queen. And then call on them when you need them. In fact, call on them BEFORE you need them – because only a Warrior would wait until she was on her knees to enlist the wisdom of others. Right?

THE MOST IMPORTANT COMPONENT

Chapter 22: Be More YOU Every Day

You might have read this whole book thinking that it's my intention to turn you into a 'cookie cutter' Queen and it's important before we finish, that we set the record straight. You see, fundamentally, at the heart of Remarkable Leadership is the core belief that the path to growth and impact is honouring *who we are* and growing from there.

All Queens are not made from the fairy tale image. I would argue that none of us are. There is no expectation that as you grow into your Queen leadership you learn to glide around a room with grace and elegance and all things flow freely. In this world there are eccentric Queens and quirky Queens. There are Rebel Queens, Revolutionary Queens and Questioning Queens and all kinds of personalities in between. What binds us together is a realisation that when we put the Warrior and Victim modes to one side, we have access to so much more. When we realise that we can drop the winning and losing game in favour of the Infinite Game, we can create new possibilities that right now seem unimaginable. When we learn to speak the truth in a way that is aligned to who we truly are and resonates with our heart as well as our head, we are able to be with other humans in fresh new ways. When we finally own that we are creating our own experience, we can laugh at the beliefs and structures we had previously held onto.

Throughout all of that, we can lead others to a similar understanding: by showing up and owning our humanity, by not pretending to be someone we are not, but instead being who we truly are, underneath all that desire to fit in. By gently and powerfully questioning the status quo and revealing new opportunities and ways of Being we can open up ways for ecosystems and organisations to be different:

more human, more creative, more heart-centred, more impactful. We can start to explore the enormity of our own potential.

So, as you explore your own Queen Leadership in the world, I invite you to pay less attention to all of the things you are not. I have never met a person yet who has managed to give themselves a personality transplant by every year insisting that they can change who they are. Instead, I invite you to pay attention to all of the things you ARE. Go deeper with those. Own your utterly unique brilliance and your quirks and foibles, and simply make the choice each day to be just a tiny bit more you than you were yesterday. There will never be another you in the whole of space and time – no one who thinks exactly the way you can or who has the exact same combination of gifts. Honour that. Explore it. Commit to your growth. For all of us. You see, in this world where we all insist on trying to be someone we are not in order to fit in, we miss out on who each and every one of us WAS BORN TO BE.

I have a funny feeling, that if we would all simply commit to showing up as our truest selves, owning our glorious potential and stepping out into the world with delight at the opportunity to create the changes we envisage, we might just find that some of the world's problems disappear. I might be wrong, of course, but it seems an exciting prospect compared with the choices we are making as a collective now.

Create your Remarkable Life and your Remarkable Leadership. There are a lot of people out there who can't wait to be led by YOU.

Emerge, Queen. We're waiting for you.

WHAT DANIELLE MACLEOD IS UP TO NOW

Remarkable Women – Women the World is Talking About

I am one of two co-founders of Remarkable Women. Alongside the outstanding talent that is Nic Devlin, we invite women who want to explore another way of living into our Communities and Programmes. Our Flagship Programme, Remarkable Leadership is attended by women from all walks of life who have a common curiosity in what is possible when we get out of our own way. Twice a year we run Emerge – the Retreat, for women who want to go deep into the ways in which they are blocking their own Queen journey. We work one to one and in small groups with women who are willing to dive into another chapter in their lives – one where their Heart and Soul have far more of a say.

It is my deep desire to live in a world of equality, fairness and love for all human beings. I believe women leaders have a huge role to play in redesigning our World Systems so that these basic human needs become available for everyone. We are a long way from getting it right, yet what I know for sure is that if each of us were willing to put our ego needs to one side in favour of living, doing and being the humanity we long to see in the world, everything would change. *It has to.*

At Remarkable Women we are calling you to grow in your own self-understanding, to deepen your awareness of how your mind plays tricks on you, to soften your eyes and your heart to the human experience and, most of all, to role model to all of the girls who are watching you, that the very best choice you can make for the world is to be yourself. They will not follow your *teaching*: they will follow your *example*.

If you'd like to explore more, go to
www.remarkablewomen.co.uk
http://www.remarkablewomen.co.uk/to discover what we're about.
Even better, write to me. Tell me who you are and what you long for. I'd love to hear from you.

Danielle #TRFOL
Danielle@remarkablewomen.co.uk

Acknowledgements

This book is dedicated to all of the Remarkable Women who have taken the Path of Queen. You have my heart, always.

My heartfelt thanks to:

Marc David, for introducing me to my inner Queen and inadvertently setting this world of Remarkable Women in motion.

Elaine Jaynes, for modelling Ruthless Compassion and showing me the path. I miss you.

My Mama, for learning to rise again.

Nic, for holding me to my promises and my dreams, and keeping me true.

And John, my King.

Lightning Source UK Ltd.
Milton Keynes UK
UKHW020701050323
418046UK00011B/1361